MICHAEL SHANKS

What's Wrong
with the
Modern World?
Agenda
for a New Society

THE BODLEY HEAD
LONDON   SYDNEY
TORONTO

For
MARK, ANDREW, JULIAN,
NEIL, HELENA, CHRISTOPHER,
FIONA, JEREMY,
AMANDA and ROLAND
who are my children and step-children,
and whose generation will have to sort
the mess out somehow

British Library Cataloguing
in Publication Data
Shanks, Michael
What's wrong with the modern world?
1. Social change
I. Title
301.24   HM101
ISBN 0-370-30101-3

© Michael Shanks 1978
Printed and bound in Great Britain for
The Bodley Head Ltd
9 Bow Street, London WC2E 7AL
by Redwood Burn Limited
Trowbridge and Esher
Set in Monotype Bembo
by Gloucester Typesetting Co. Ltd
First published 1978

Contents

Things fall apart; the centre cannot hold;
Mere anarchy is loosed upon the world,
The blood-dimmed tide is loosed, and everywhere
The ceremony of innocence is drowned;
The best lack all conviction, while the worst
Are full of passionate intensity.

    W. B. YEATS, *The Second Coming*

Preface

Between June 1973 and January 1976 I was working in the European Commission in Brussels, as director-general for social affairs. On my return to the United Kingdom I was commissioned to write two books, both of which appeared in 1977. The first, *European Social Policy, Today and Tomorrow*, sought to draw the lessons from my experiences in Brussels. The second, *Planning and Politics: The British Experience 1960–76*, analysed the history of economic planning in the U K over the past fifteen years, and probed the reasons for the meagre results obtained. In writing these two books, I became aware of a number of aspects of our recent and present troubles which seemed to go beyond the scope of either book, and to have general application for the future of our civilisation. In trying to follow these leads, I found myself writing a third book, to which I gave the possibly tendentious title, *What's Wrong with the Modern World?* Here it is.

The interaction between economic and social policy has always fascinated me. My first book, *The Stagnant Society*, first published in 1961, tried to explain the reasons for Britain's very poor rate of economic growth by reference to the class divisions in British society, and their impact on trade union attitudes and industrial relations. This thesis, regarded as eccentric at the time, has now become widely accepted, especially by foreign observers of the British scene. In *The Innovators* (1967) I analysed the impact of technological innovation on society, and the elements in the social structure which facilitated or obstructed innovation.

Both these books were written with special reference to the U K. This one is not. During the period when it was being written Britain was going through an exceptionally traumatic and introverted period (from which it now seems happily to be emerging). In these circumstances it would have been tempting to focus on the special problems of the U K economy. But my years in Brussels taught me that the problems facing the major countries of the west arise from similar causes, and that there is nothing unique about the situation of Britain or any other one country. This book therefore deals with the problems of western civilisation as a whole—though admittedly more from a European than a transatlantic viewpoint—treating the problems of individual countries only to make points of general application.

However, if the problems—of inflation, unemployment and swollen public sectors—are common to all western countries, some have coped with them much better than others. The U S, Germany and Switzerland have consistently kept their rate of inflation well below the world rate, while the U K and Italy have been consistently above. This discrepancy, which in a relatively free trading world feeds through very rapidly to comparative costs, and thus to the balance of world trade, has been a major disequilibrating factor in the world scene, leading to a growing division in the industrial world between strong and weak economies. (Japan, with high domestic inflation rates but a protected home market, has proved an exception to this general rule, reemerging after the initial shock of the 1973 oil price explosion as one of the perennially strong economies. North Sea oil is in process of making Great Britain another exception, ensuring a strong balance of payments despite high inflation.) The thesis of this book is that, at least in Europe, the countries which have weathered the economic storm best are normally those with the healthiest social structures.

It occurred to me, when writing my book about U K economic planning, that if one-tenth of the effort devoted to economic planning over the past fifteen years had been devoted instead to social planning, our economic structure would almost certainly be a lot stronger today. In this book I try to explain why.

This book covers a wide field, linking a number of different disciplines usually kept separate in our over-compartmentalised intellectual world. Consequently the argument is often rather condensed. However, I have tried to avoid jargon, and the book

is designed to be read by the non-specialist. I hope I have succeeded.

If I have, it is in large measure due to Graham Bannock and
Richard Hauser, who read the book in draft and made a number
of helpful suggestions. They are in no way to blame for any errors
which remain, either of fact or interpretation.

My thanks are also due to Betty Stuart, for invaluable secretarial
help in connection with all three of the books written since my
return from Brussels.

But above all I would like to thank all the fellow-citizens with
whom I have had the privilege of working, over the years, in the
U K and abroad. It is to them I owe such insights as I have been
able to acquire about the nature of the society in which we live,
and the civilisation of which we are the heirs and trustees. Our
inheritance is a not ignoble one, and I trust that when the history
of our times comes to be written we will be found not unworthy
of it. More than that, no mortal can claim.

One final word. Since this book went to the printer, I was
appointed chairman of the National Consumer Council. I have
made no alterations to the text on this account, nor have I discussed the book with any of my colleagues on the Council. Neither
the brief references to consumerism, nor any other aspects of the
book, can be taken to reflect the views of the Council, nor indeed
of anybody but myself.

MJS
December, 1977

I

The Keynesian Legacy

About a sixth of the way through *Tender Is The Night*, Scott Fitzgerald's tragic semi-autobiographical novel written in the early 1930s, the hero Dick Diver takes a party of fellow-Americans on a tour of the First World War battlefields. Looking across the Somme he says: 'See that little stream—we could walk to it in two minutes. It took the British a month to walk to it—a whole empire walking very slowly, dying in front and pushing forward behind. And another empire walked very slowly backward a few inches a day, leaving the dead like a million bloody rugs. No Europeans will ever do that again in this generation . . . This took religion and years of plenty and tremendous sureties and the exact relation that existed between the classes . . . You had to have a whole-souled sentimental equipment going back further than you could remember. You had to remember Christmas, and postcards of the Crown Prince and his fiancée, and little cafés in Valence and beer gardens in Unter den Linden and weddings at the *mairie*, and going to the Derby, and your grandfather's whiskers . . . This kind of battle was invented by Lewis Carroll and Jules Verne and whoever wrote *Undine*, and country deacons bowling and *marraines* in Marseilles and girls seduced in the back lanes of Württemburg and Westphalia. Why, this was a love battle—there was a century of middle-class love spent here . . . All my beautiful lovely safe world blew itself up here with a great gust of high explosive love.'

Of course, in one sense Fitzgerald was wrong. Europe *was* to repeat the carnage again in his generation, though in a different form. But in a deeper sense he was right. A social and political order *did* destroy itself between 1914 and 1918, as a result of the cumulative undercurrents of a century of bourgeois civilisation.

The attempt to put the pieces together again at the Treaty of Versailles failed, both politically and economically; this failure was followed by the great depression, the Third Reich, and a second world war. After 1945 a new world order was constructed, based very largely on the ideas of the great English economist, J. M. Keynes.

That world order in turn is now threatened—not by national rivalries as in 1914, but more by the kinds of subliminal changes in our culture hinted at by Scott Fitzgerald in that (to me at any rate) marvellously evocative passage. What this book seeks to do is to record and analyse the forces battering at the Keynesian world order established after the Second World War, and to suggest ways in which the system can be modified to accommodate these forces and preserve our threatened civilisation.

It has been said that all western philosophy consists of footnotes to Plato. It could be argued with more justice that all post-1945 economics consists of footnotes to Keynes. There has seldom been so total a capture of the citadels of power by a thinker in the modern world as the Keynesian takeover of the capitalist system (the nearest parallel is Marx's domination of the other half of the industrialised world).

Keynes: The Man and the System

John Maynard (later Lord) Keynes, born in Cambridge in 1883, was a thinker and man of affairs in the great English liberal tradition, and one of the greatest economists of all time—equalled perhaps only by Adam Smith and Karl Marx. Like them, he was an economics polymath (perhaps the last we shall ever see, given the increasing complexity of the discipline); but, like them, his interests went beyond political economy to encompass the broader purposes of society. Re-reading his work thirty years after his death, one is acutely conscious of the narrowing of perspective which has accompanied the increasing specialisation and obsession with technique of his successors. Not only did Keynes move easily in the worlds of academics, politics and banking; 'he loved philosophy and farming, paintings and the ballet, old books and modern poetry'.[1] The modern world sadly misses this kind of breadth of vision among its gurus and advisers.

Keynes's seminal writing was done in the late 1920s and early 1930s. Had his theories been accepted then, rather than in the 1940s, the world might have avoided the great slump. For Keynes discovered the overriding importance in economic systems of *demand*. It is clear that economic stability can only be reached if demand and supply are in approximate balance; it did not need Keynes to teach the world that. But the essence of the Keynesian message was that demand and supply could be balanced at very different levels of activity, and that governments had the ability, and the responsibility, to see that the level of demand was such as to keep the productive resources of the economy fully employed in meeting it.

The chief function of government, therefore, in the economic sphere was *demand management*. If the demand for goods and services was greater than the resources available to supply them, the result would be inflation, as potential buyers bid up prices by trying to secure their share of a limited supply. This would apply whether the commodity in short supply was a material (oil, food, motor-cars) or labour. Normally, of course, the two would go together. If there was an excess demand for goods or services, entrepreneurs would be eager to make a profit by making more— and for that they would need more labour, to build the plant and make the goods.

In such circumstances the role of government should be to restrain demand, by taking money out of circulation. This it could do by either *fiscal* means (running a budget surplus by raising more money in taxes than it needed to finance its own spending) or *monetary* means (making borrowing more expensive by raising interest rates, or on occasion preventing banks from lending money). A third possible line of attack would be to restrict wage increases by legislation or political pressure. Since wages and salaries normally make up around two-thirds of national income, the higher wages and salaries go the more spending power is available in the community, and therefore the worse inflation is likely to get.

If on the other hand—as was normally the case between the wars—effective demand is not enough to put all available resources to work, the function of government should be to increase demand by putting more money into circulation. The crudest way of doing this is simply by printing money. Another way is to put unemployed people to work on public works projects and the like, and pay them wages. The third and fourth ways are by inverting the fiscal and monetary policies described in the last paragraph. Thus the government can put money into circulation by spending more than it raises in taxes—because government IOUs are normally accepted as legal tender (this is, if you like, another way of printing money). Similarly it can make borrowing cheaper by lowering interest rates—and, if banks and other private money-lenders are not willing to co-operate, it can go into the market itself by lending its own money cheaply.

Thus it came to be accepted after 1945 that a government in a western capitalist country could and should so manage its affairs that it achieved full employment, stable prices and a reasonable rate of economic growth, by developing the techniques of demand management briefly indicated above. Of course it would have to take account of fluctuations in business activity due to the effects of the trade cycle, movements in commodity prices, fluctuations in international trade and so on. But this could be done by continuously altering the regulators of the economy—the incidence of taxation, the rate of interest for borrowing, public spending etc.—to offset the fluctuations from outside. This came to be known as 'fine-tuning'.

However, no country can insulate itself from the affairs of others, and a country which continually ran its economy at a higher level of activity than others would be liable to encounter difficulties in its balance of payments. Part of the high demand for goods and services in such a country would be met by imports. If there was a heavy demand for goods and services for the home market there would be less available to be sold abroad to pay for the imports. The higher the rate of activity the greater likelihood of wages and prices being bid up, so that the country's goods and services would cost more abroad and be less competitive. So, as the experience of the 1930s showed, it was very difficult for one country or a small group of countries to aim at full employment policies if others, within a world of relatively free trade, did not do likewise. Countries trying to balance their books abroad by deflating could easily export depression to their trading partners, leading either to a cumulative world slump, or to the spread of autarky and protectionism as countries sought to preserve their economies from the contagion of 'beggar-my-neighbour' deflationary policies by restricting foreign imports and mounting siege economies.

Both of these were anathema to the liberal-oriented governments emerging from the rubble of 1945. And so a world economic order was constructed on Keynesian principles (mainly at the 1944 Bretton Woods conference), under which the leading western economies pledged themselves to policies of full employment at home and liberal trading systems abroad. If any country found itself in balance of payments difficulties it was entitled to borrow money from a new institution, the International Monetary Fund (IMF), to which all had subscribed. If it still found itself uncompetitive, the best solution would be for it to lower its exchange rate *vis-à-vis* other countries, thus automatically lowering its prices on world markets; similarly, a country with a persistent balance of payments surplus should raise its exchange rate, thus making its goods more expensive. But before this was done, recourse should be had to all the devices of 'fine-tuning' to correct external imbalances. Thus a country in deficit abroad should raise its interest rates to attract foreign money, should take steps to reduce the level of activity at home (but not to the point of 'beggar-my-neighbour' deflation), and so on. Temporary imbalances should be dealt with in short by methods of demand management, structural imbalances by variations in exchange rates (devaluation or revaluation, or letting the currency 'float' on international exchange markets until it found a naturally stable level).

To a remarkable extent, this system (of which the account given here is of necessity extremely streamlined and over-simplified) worked for the first two post-war decades. During these twenty years western countries enjoyed the greatest boom, the most sustained period of economic growth, that the world has ever seen. Full employment was by and large achieved (though with a number of imperfections, as we shall see later). World trade, and the interdependence of economies, developed as never before. Prices tended to rise year by year, but at a modest and tolerable rate. Wages, salaries and other incomes rose faster, reflecting full employment and rapid increases in productivity (resulting from improvements in technology), so that the standard of living of the great mass of people in the advanced industrial countries—Europe, North America, Japan, Australasia—advanced at a rate unprecedented in human history.

The Onset of Inflation

Future historians may look back on the Age of Keynes, as Gibbon in *The Decline and Fall of the Roman Empire* did on the Age of the Antonines, as 'the period in the history of the world, during which the condition of the human race was most happy and prosperous'—rather than to that Edwardian evening, before the holocaust, celebrated by Scott Fitzgerald in the quotation which begins this book. I do not know. It is too early to say. But what is clear is that, somewhere around the middle to late 1960s, something started to go badly wrong. The mould began to break. The 'fine-tuners' lost control of the machine. And, ten years later, we are scrambling about in the ruins trying to recreate a world order which we only imperfectly understand.

What went wrong? In trying to piece together a complex series of structures, one has to start with a single, comprehensible point—a point which, if grasped, may illuminate other elements. The simplest way to explain the break-up of the Keynesian system is to say that inflation got out of control. In the period between the early 1960s and the early 1970s the average annual rate of price increase throughout the western world jumped from around $2\frac{1}{2}\%$ to around $12\frac{1}{2}\%$—in some countries, including the

UK, substantially more. How did this happen? Why? And what have been the effects?

In Keynesian economics, inflation results from an excess of demand over supply. One would expect the price of a commodity to rise sharply if, and only if, people wanted more of it than was available. This could happen for one of two reasons. The demand could increase because people became richer and wanted to spend some of their increased income on the commodity in question; or because there was a switch of consumer preference away from other commodities or savings in favour of this particular commodity, which could arise from a skilful marketing policy or technological developments, or simply from changes in fashion or customer tastes. Alternatively, supply could fall below the level of demand because of natural causes (the failure of a crop due to adverse weather conditions, for example); or because monopoly suppliers deliberately kept supply down in order to boost prices and profits. A general prolonged rise in prices such as occurred in the late 1960s could not, by definition, reflect changes in preferences between commodities, nor would it be likely to reflect deliberate restrictions in supply. Thus it would most likely reflect a general increase in demand resulting from rises in incomes, and therefore spending power.

Why would incomes rise in the Keynesian system? Given that the great majority of incomes consist of wages and salaries, the answer is that they will probably rise for exactly the same reasons as other prices; for wages and salaries are the price at which the crucial factor of labour is bought and sold. Wages and salaries may be expected to rise, therefore, when there is a shortage of labour relative to the demand for it. Such a shortage tends to occur when either or both the following features are present: a rapidly-growing economy, with high levels of prosperity and therefore a growing demand for industry's products, requiring the input of more labour to satisfy it; and/or restrictions, or the threat of restrictions, on the supply of labour by institutions (typically trade unions) which control it.

Thus, one would expect prices and incomes to move upwards

together in periods of high economic activity. A rise in incomes will create increased purchasing power, thus stimulating demand for goods and services, and also—for that reason—demand for more labour. At the same time a rise in wages[2] will increase industry's costs, thereby requiring offsetting rises in price if the business sector is to remain profitable. But rising prices will themselves stimulate demands for higher incomes, to counteract the increase in living costs. So it is not difficult to see how an inflationary spiral can develop in a capitalist system, given a high level of demand, whether the spiral starts by increases in prices or by increases in wages and salaries.

In the post-war period, inflationary pressures have tended to come from the wages rather than from the prices side in most cases. There have been some dramatic exceptions, such as the boom in commodity prices at the time of the Korean war in 1950; or, most remarkably, the fourfold increase in oil prices imposed by the Organisation of Petroleum Exporting Countries (OPEC), the cartel of oil exporting nations, in 1973. This was a classic example of monopolistic price exploitation. But such cases have been rare in the post-war era. This is partly because, in a relatively free-trading world, and one where technological innovation has eroded former product monopolies by discovering substitutes, the ability of a single supplier or a small group of suppliers to hold the customer to ransom is limited by competition (if not by the actions of government). But it also reflects the fact that businessmen have been able, for most of the time, to absorb material cost increases by greater efficiency—output per worker has been growing at an annual rate of between $2\frac{1}{2}\%$ and 4% over most of the western world over the period as a whole—and by increasing sales volume. By and large, it has paid businessmen to follow strategies of high sales volume rather than high unit prices.

The same restraining factors have not occurred to anything like the same extent on the side of incomes, however. We have to note there are significant differences between wages and other kinds of price. Wages have, as already noted, a dual function in the economy. They are the price a worker receives for his or her labour. They are also the main element of spending in the economy, making up as they do the greater part of national income. This has a very fundamental consequence. As we have seen, in buoyant trade conditions the same basic factors push wages and prices up together, the one reinforcing the other. But in slack conditions, while prices can and should be allowed to fall, to bring supply and demand into balance, it is both dangerous and impracticable to treat wages in the same way; for this can cause a cumulative downward spiral in economic activity, the exact inverse of the inflationary upward spiral to which I have already alluded.

Keynes established this proposition conclusively when he argued, at the beginning of his most important book *The General Theory of Employment, Interest and Money*, that trade unions were behaving rationally when—contrary to the received wisdom of the day—they insisted on maintaining wages at a time of depression and unemployment. According to the classical economists the price of labour, like any other price, should be allowed to fall to the level at which demand would equal supply. Not so, said Keynes; for the price of labour itself helps to determine the demand. If workers' wages fall, they will have less to spend, so the level of demand throughout the economy will fall further, putting more jobs at risk. By maintaining wages, and thus purchasing power, workers limit the fall in the economy, other things being equal.

There are other reasons why, in practice, wages are more 'sticky' than most kinds of prices. There is a strong *institutional* element in wage determination. Minimum wages are often the subject of governmental edict, being decided on social rather than economic criteria. (If wages fall below subsistence level, government would have to make up the difference anyway, out of its welfare budget. So on pragmatic as well as political and social grounds, governments have an interest in seeing minimum wages kept above subsistence level.) In industries where there is strong union organisation, basic wages and conditions are normally settled at an industry-wide level between central bargainers representing worker and employer interests, rather than by face-to-face haggling between individual buyers and sellers of labour. (Very often, of course, local variations on top of the centrally negotiated basic agreements are settled on the spot between individual employers and individual workers or small groups of workers. Thus, while basic wages are determined by overall bargaining strength and skill, local variations in the demand-and-supply relationship are reflected in the individual shopfloor negotiations, which typically cover such things as over-time arrangements, local 'fringe benefits', and other elements known to economists as 'wage drift'. Thus it is untrue to suggest that wage movements are entirely unresponsive to changes in market conditions, though institutional factors blunt and blur the relationship.)

The institutional element in wage bargaining is strengthened by other factors too. Because trade unions number among their members a substantial proportion of the total electorate, and because their power to order a withdrawal of labour in support of their claims or grievances can directly affect the economy, they can muster much *political* support for their claims irrespective of the strength of demand for their members' services. By the same token, governments cannot avoid being concerned with the out-come of the major wage negotiations, simply because of the large numbers of people involved. An agreement covering several millions of workers may result in a wage increase which to each individual recipient is very modest; but the effect on the economy as a whole is bound to be significant.

Thus the determination of wage levels cannot in practice follow the same rules as the determination of other prices. The relation-ship to supply and demand is both more distant and more com-plex. There is the fact that recipients of wages are *people*, with rights and votes; that they are typically organised in *unions*, which have a certain degree of monopoly bargaining power; and that very frequently governments become involved as third parties in major wage negotiations. Finally, there is the complication that wages help to *determine* the level of demand, as well as *reflecting* it.

Inflation in the Keynesian Era

During the Keynesian era economists were becoming more and more concerned about the possibility of these factors, combined with governments' commitment to full employment—which in a sense underpins trade union bargaining strength—creating a permanent tendency towards inflation: inflation caused, not so much by the suction effect of excess demand, as by the upward pressure of unions on costs. This was called 'cost-push' inflation, as opposed to the orthodox 'demand-pull' inflation identified by Keynes. Thus, by pushing up labour costs trade unions could force firms to raise prices, generating an inflationary wage/price spiral irrespective of the level of overall demand (and helping to sustain it once started, through the extra purchasing power created by the wage rises). As we have seen, 'cost-push' pressures could—and sometimes did—originate in the actions of monopoly suppliers of goods and services, eager to expand profits; but, for the reasons we have seen, these were normally easier to counteract than union wage pressures.

Keynesian economics did not provide any immediate antidote to 'cost-push' inflation. If governments reacted to rising prices throughout the economy by trying to reduce demand, the first results could be counter-productive. Workers would feel themselves worse off, because their wage increases would be offset, not only by higher prices, but also by higher taxes and/or higher interest rates on their borrowing; earnings from overtime would fall, some of them would be put on short-time work, some might even become unemployed. Those still at work would try to compensate by demanding still higher wages. Firms on the other hand would find that they could not recoup their increased labour or material costs by high sales volume in a market deliberately depressed by government's 'fine-tuning'. So they would be forced to raise unit prices still higher to cover increased costs on smaller sales volume.

Thus for a time at least the spiral could get worse, as the level of activity declined. But, on Keynesian arguments, this could not last for ever—provided governments kept their nerve, and were prepared to see firms go bankrupt and unemployment rise. Sooner or later there must come an equilibrium point at which cost pressures would die out in a demand vacuum; a time must arrive when the ability of unions to press successfully for higher wages would be countered by the inability of firms to pay, and the fear of loss of jobs.

In Keynesian terms the issue was much more one of politics than of economics, the key variables being the readiness of government to face a confrontation with the unions, and to allow sectors of industry to go to the wall, and the policy priorities of the trade unions themselves. But an important part of neo-Keynesian analysis in the post-war period was devoted to identifying the economic conditions which would enable full employment (however defined) to be maintained without generating inflation. Some economists argued for institutionalised incomes policies, by which unions could be persuaded not to exercise their full bargaining power in order to maintain economic stability. (This subject recurs later in the book, particularly in Chapter 8.)

Other Keynesians—notably Professors Paish and Phillips in the United Kingdom—tried to identify conditions in which an equilibrium could be maintained between 'cost-push' and demand factors. They argued that there must be a level of demand at which union pressures for wage increases would be effectively neutralised by workers' fear of increasing unemployment and employers' fear of losing sales if prices were increased. Thus Professor Paish recommended that the government should ensure through its demand-management policies that a certain reserve of unused capacity and unemployed workers should be maintained, as a kind of deterrent against excessive wage pressure and economic 'overheating'. Professor Phillips established, as a result of statistical studies in the UK over a long period, that there was a definite correlation between rates of unemployment and wage stability. The higher the unemployment, the lower the rate of wage increase. Thus the object of economic policy should be to run the economy at such a level of activity that wages would rise in line with, but not more than, the natural increase in productivity and business efficiency. In these circumstances prices and profits would remain stable.

It must be stressed that for both Paish and Phillips the equilibrium level of unemployment, the level at which wages would rise no faster than productivity, came within the conventional definition of 'full employment', which was officially defined in the UK as less than 3% of the working population out of work. For both of them the equilibrium level fluctuated, depending on external circumstances, between $1\frac{1}{2}\%$ and $2\frac{1}{2}\%$ unemployed. It was within these parameters that the government should operate its 'fine-tuning' mechanisms, depressing demand when union wage pressures were most acute and/or when underlying trading conditions were most buoyant, allowing it to expand a little— but never below the 'danger level' of $1\frac{1}{2}\%$ unemployment—when conditions were slacker and unions more quiescent; governments, in short, should always be 'leaning against the wind' in their economic policies.

The 'Phillips curve', which identified the precise trade-off points between rates of unemployment and rates of wage increase, proved a remarkably useful tool of economic management until the late 1960s. Throughout the two decades of the Age of Keynes, governments in the western world proved highly successful at combining full employment, fast rates of economic growth and relative—though not absolute—price stability. But from about 1968 onwards the situation began to change—slowly at first, then dramatically. Inflation rates began to accelerate at the same time as unemployment was rising. The equilibrium point on the 'Phillips curve' started to move sharply to the right of the graph—in other words, to higher and higher unemployment levels. Indeed, it came to seem that there was almost no point at which unemployment would be severe enough to destroy the bargaining power of trade unions or their determination to win wage increases; or, if there was such a point, it could never be discovered empirically because no government would dare to deflate the economy far enough to identify it, for fear of generating a total social collapse.

The Monetarist Theory

Thus, as the familiar Keynesian relationships began to disappear from the landscape, economists started to grope around with increasing desperation for explanations. One such explanation for the take-off in inflation rates in the late 1960s, at a time of weak economic demand in the world as a whole and rising rates of unemployment, is contained in the theories of the so-called 'monetarists'. The most important monetarist economist is without doubt Professor Milton Friedman of Chicago University (though there are monetarists of an earlier vintage in Europe, notably Jacques Rueff in France, whose thinking greatly influenced General de Gaulle). Monetarism is an extremely simple concept in principle, though highly complex in detail. The basic tenet is that inflation is a function, not of the demand for goods and services, but of the supply of money. Governments create or facilitate inflation by expanding the money supply. This was impossible in the days before 1914 when money in domestic circulation was normally backed by gold; the money supply was not in those days under the control of governments. In the international sphere this situation continued throughout the inter-war period, and in a modified form into the 1960s. National currency reserves had to be related to the amount of gold held in national vaults. This imposed a discipline on governments, which throughout this century has been progressively relaxed as gold has been phased out of the monetary system—first domestically, then internationally. Today the standard of value, both domestically and internationally, is a man-made currency—paper money. The more that governments create, naturally, the more its value declines in relation to the things that it buys. Thus, unless governments replace the automatic discipline imposed by the gold standard by an equal self-imposed discipline, inflation is inevitable —and it will grow fastest in those countries where resort to the printing press is easiest.

Beyond any question, as we shall see, the lack of discipline on the part of governments with regard to the money supply has been one element in the inflationary upsurge. But in most cases it has been, in my view, a secondary factor. One has to ask why governments have expanded the money supply, in knowledge of the risks they were running. Clearly they did it in response to external pressures. We have to ask ourselves what was the nature of those pressures, and why they could not be resisted.

Trigger Points for Inflation

One part of the answer lies in the special situation confronting the United States government in the mid-1960s, during the presidency of Lyndon Johnson. The government was fighting a war in Vietnam which was both costly and unpopular. At the same time it was undertaking a very expensive domestic programme of social expenditure, entitled the 'Great Society'. It could not finance both out of its current income, nor did it dare to raise new taxes for the Vietnam war—which it might not have been able to get through Congress anyway. Faced with the classic choice between guns or butter—the war or the welfare programme—it decided to do both, financing the war by borrowing on government IOUs, which became in effect convertible currency.

Thus during the mid-1960s the world became awash with dollars. Some of these dollars—the so-called 'Eurodollars'—were used to help finance US overseas investment, notably in western Europe. The US was in a better position than most countries to print money, because the dollar had long been accepted as the world's major reserve currency, so that dollar IOUs were universally acceptable. The only thing which had to be done to remove all external constraints on the US printing presses was to cut the link with gold—i.e. the arrangement by which gold and dollars were freely exchangeable at a fixed rate—and this was duly done in the 1968 Washington agreement.

Thus one of the trigger points for the great inflation of the late 1960s and early 1970s was the decision of the US government to expand the domestic money supply to meet its commitments, and the readiness of the rest of the world to accept dollar IOUs—in other words, to allow the US to run massive payments deficits on its foreign account.

But there were other trigger points of a different nature. In Paris in May 1968 there was a massive wave of student riots, in protest at university conditions; the protest rapidly expanded into an attack on the way in which the Gaullist regime was running France. In a matter of days the unrest spread to industry. Workers downed tools in what soon became virtually a general strike. France seemed to be on the verge of revolution. But the government reacted swiftly. The students were suppressed, often brutally (though some of their specific demands for reform of the university system were later met). The workers were bought off by their employers, with government approval, by what at the time seemed remarkably high wage increases, averaging around 16%.

A third trigger point, of a different nature and less dramatic than these two, was the way in which the UK decimalised its currency in 1966. The then Chancellor of the Exchequer, James Callaghan, was faced with two alternative ways of 'going decimal'. The first option was to make the main unit the existing ten shillings. If there were to be a hundred new pennies to this new main unit, the new penny would be worth 1.2 old pennies. The second option was to base the new decimal currency on the existing pound, which would mean that the new penny would be worth 2.4 old pennies. Those concerned with fighting inflation in the UK urged the Chancellor to go for the first option, arguing that otherwise there would be an irresistible tendency to 'round up' prices expressed in pennies, and that this would work its way right through the system. The Bank of England on the other hand insisted that the prestige and standing of the pound should be maintained (whatever that might mean in practice as opposed to rhetoric!), and that the second option should therefore be preferred. The Chancellor bowed to City advice. Subsequent evidence suggests that those of us who argued that this would have long-term inflationary consequences were not overstating our case.

However, isolated if significant events of the kind indicated above could not have produced the consequences that they did had there not been other forces at work. They were in effect sparks which served to ignite the dry tinder lying around. But why was the tinder dry?

It is at this point that the economists cease to give us much guidance, and we have to turn instead to broader and deeper currents within contemporary society and culture—to the kind of things listed by Dick Diver in his elegy to the pre-1914 *ancien régime* with which this chapter began.

The Keynesian system, like the earlier classical economic system, relied on certain disciplines to maintain balance. These disciplines were exercised through the demand-management devices of 'fine-tuning'. The basic difference between the Keynesian order and the classical order which had preceded it was that in the latter the disciplines were automatic—the 'hidden hand' extolled by Adam Smith in *The Wealth of Nations*—whereas in the former they were exercised by governments. Under the classical order the volume of economic activity was in effect regulated by the supply of money, which was in turn largely a function of the amount of gold discovered and produced. Under the Keynesian order the volume of activity was a function of government policy, printing presses having replaced goldmines as the major source of money.

Obviously governments find it more difficult and unrewarding to depress activity than to stimulate it, so that there has been throughout the Keynesian era a built-in tendency for governments to err on the inflationary side in their 'fine-tuning' activities. (One should also not forget the role of high military spending throughout the post-war period—not only in special circumstances like those of the Vietnam war—in boosting inflation.) But for the first two post-war decades, at the cost of a 'creeping' inflation of perhaps 2–3% a year, western governments were, by and large, able to keep their economies on an even keel, with full employment and high rates of economic growth. At some point in the late 1960s the pressures suddenly intensified and governments found it impossible to maintain the disciplines. What was happening in western society to make it, quite suddenly, almost ungovernable in Keynesian terms?

NOTES TO CHAPTER 1

[1] Michael Stewart, *Keynes and After* (Penguin 1967).

[2] Wages and salaries make up by far the biggest element in incomes, and statistically wages are much more important than salaries. In this book I have therefore tended to use the word 'wages' from time to time as a shorthand term for 'wages and salaries'.

2

The World We Have Lost

The society celebrated by Dick Diver differed little, in certain fundamental respects, from that which had existed for many centuries in western Europe (and, in the Mediterranean basin, for millennia). This society contained several vital binding agents which gave it coherence and continuity, and an internal discipline. One such agent was the superior coercive power of the State. Whether the State was an absolute monarchy, a parliamentary democracy, a military dictatorship, an oligarchy or a revolutionary committee, it normally possessed the means to impose its will on its subjects. It was not always so. In every country there were periods of civil war, unrest or breakdown of law and order, but these were exceptions to normality. In the Middle Ages many of the barons had more effective power than their nominal overlords. But from the sixteenth century onwards, throughout Europe the central authorities were increasingly to tighten their hold over rebellious or over-mighty subjects. Thus there existed in every western European country a balance of power, sometimes disturbed, which nevertheless ensured the maintenance of law and order in normal times.

Behind the façade of temporal power there lay the more basic binding agent of accepted social hierarchy based on religion—what Dick Diver described as 'the exact relation that existed between the classes'. Like the political structure, the social order was not immutable. People could and did move from one class to another, and in times of social upheaval ruling classes could be and were displaced. But, once again, these were exceptional occurrences. For most of the time, most people accepted that they would occupy for all their lives a certain position in the social

31

hierarchy, and that there would be gross inequalities in wealth, power and privilege between the various levels in the hierarchy. They accepted it, essentially, for two reasons. The first was that it had the sanction of religion. The Christian Church taught obedience to the established order (within which it was strongly entrenched, and from which it derived great power, wealth and privilege). This is not to say that the Church was always a friend of despots. For most (not all) of the time it tried to influence the secular authority to exercise power in a humane, civilised and orderly way—and it did of course provide a ladder by which able children of poor people could rise in the social hierarchy. But it had no interest in the overthrow of the established order. It could and sometimes did support reform; never—if one excludes the special case of the religious wars—revolution.

Moreover, the Christian religion taught that, if social justice could not be obtained for all in this life, this was merely a delaying factor. For all who led virtuous lives in this world could be assured of perfect justice and the achievement of all their (respectable) ambitions in the after-life. In this belief people could afford to be patient in enduring poverty, privation and frustration in a world which was, after all, only an ante-chamber to the eternal. Indeed, if one believed this, any other kind of behaviour in this life would be counter-productive, for it could jeopardise one's chances of eternal happiness. It was not therefore the responsibility of the State to ensure social justice—though the nearer it could get to it the more meritorious it would be; but the ultimate responsibility in this domain, as in all others, lay with God.

It is impossible, in my view, to overstate the importance of religion in explaining the motivations and behaviour of European society up to this century. But there was another important cement for the social order—the limited horizons open to the great mass of people. By and large, most people's ambitions were limited to that whereof they had personal knowledge. If a man could live a little better than his father, or his neighbour, he had attained the summit of realisable ambition. It was pointless for Lazarus to envy or emulate Dives. There was no way, in normal circumstances, in which he could hope to replace Dives or emulate his life-style. More importantly, perhaps, he had little or no opportunity, before the advent of mass transport and mass communications, of knowing what that life-style was. What the eye does not see, the heart cannot grieve for. And so the conflicts and tensions of European society took place within the relatively narrow circle of those who were already in, or very close to, the ruling orders. The fatalism of the masses was broken only on relatively rare occasions, when famine or other disasters threatened a total breakdown and drove men to desperation, or by a particularly charismatic or apocalyptic rabble-rouser.

There were other influences making for social cohesion and discipline. Sexual morality was enforced by the fear of illegitimacy. Society was cruel to bastards and even more so to their mothers. The family thus remained the norm, the basic cell of western society; and, at the cost of personal unhappiness for the many trapped in loveless marriages, it acted as one of the great unifying and stabilising elements in society.

The Erosion of Fatalism

This basic system of sticks and carrots inducing acquiescence in the established social order and social behaviour—religion, the temporal power of the State, ignorance, intolerance of illegitimacy —was not much changed by the first century of the industrial revolution, traumatic though its effects on society were. The new industrial proletariat retained, overwhelmingly, the religious and moral beliefs of the peasant communities from whence they came. There was widespread acceptance that the wealth of industrial society could only come from the toil of the masses, and thus that any attempt to alleviate working conditions—to relieve the burden of pollution, to make work itself more attractive, less dirty and dangerous, less boring and stultifying, more democratic in its organisation and determination—would be counterproductive, because it would limit the wealth of the community, and thus ultimately of the workers themselves. This was the price that had to be paid for progress.

However, it was the industrial revolution and the new organis-ational structures it brought with it, science and technology, which were to subvert each of the binding agents of European society, one by one. The political balance of power was to be profoundly influenced by two developments—the spread of universal suffrage (only finally achieved in most western societies during this century), and the growth of trade unions, who were to become in the post-1945 period 'over-mighty subjects' capable of challenging and overruling the established power of the State. The new scientific discoveries, particularly those of Charles Darwin, were to erode the spiritual authority of the Christian Church (already challenged by the eighteenth-century enlightenment)—faster in urban societies than in rural ones, more lethally in Protestant than in Catholic communities—until, by the middle of the twentieth century, belief in an after-life had ceased to be a major motivating factor among the mass of the people in any western country.

At least as important was the effect of modern technology in enlarging people's knowledge of how others lived, in widening their horizons and increasing their ambitions. With the invention of the railway, then the motor-car and finally the aeroplane, people achieved a physical mobility hitherto undreamed of. With the radio, the cinema and then television, people became aware to a vastly greater extent than ever before of the realities of the world beyond their immediate neighbourhood. One of the unfortunate aspects of the new enlightenment was its use by producers of mass consumer goods as a device for stimulating demand. It was inevitable that industrialists would see in the mass media a marvellous marketing tool to increase awareness of their products and to create new demands for them. Thus a very substantial part of the images conveyed on TV screens throughout the world has come to consist of messages designed to make people dissatisfied with what they have and determined to get more. Television has made people better informed; it has also set out to, and has been able to, make them in general less satisfied and more envious.

Even more significant have been the effects of medical techno-logy. The invention of safe, easy methods of contraception has broken the previous link between promiscuity and illegitimacy. No longer is a bastard child the inevitable and unconcealable evidence of impermissible sexual intercourse. As a result, illegitimacy is no longer the social stigma that it was, since it can be assumed to be the result of a conscious choice (though it may be carelessness) on the part of the mother, rather than involuntary evidence of guilt.

The result has been what is called the 'permissive society'—a society in which the nuclear marriage is no longer the unquestioned norm, in which sexual freedom and sexual experimentation are exercised openly to an extent probably unparalleled in Christian civilisation, and in which the gulf between the 'liberated' young and their parents seems to have replaced some of the previous class-based stratifications of society.

There are other important factors at work in accentuating the 'generation gap' in western society. One has been the emergence of young people as a newly affluent consumer market with special characteristics and with very large collective purchasing power. This has led to the development of a specific 'pop culture', with its own ethos and with heavy sales promotion of its main products; alongside this development has gone an uglier form of commercial exploitation in the form of an international market in drugs aimed at the young. A second factor, of great importance, was the enormous development of higher education which took place in all western countries during the late 1950s and early 1960s. The object of this expansion was to provide the human capital for a new economic leap forward into an age of high technology and automation; but the effects so far have been rather different.

The new generation of highly educated youth are, in general, critical of the life-styles prevalent in their societies. They set a high value on self-expression and individual freedom—'doing your own thing'—and a low value on conformity and authority. The 1968 student revolt in France was only the most spectacular of a whole series of student protest movements which took place in all the main western democracies during the late 1960s and early 1970s.

The challenge to authority is accompanied by a much more critical approach to the costs of economic growth—whether the costs are *external* in the sense of the harm done to the outside environment, or *internal* in the sense of the working methods and conditions employed to produce the goods. This has led to new demands of various kinds being made on industry.

Throughout the capitalist era there has of course been an undercurrent of concern about the effects of industrialisation on society. The nineteenth century saw a steady sharpening of the social conscience, beginning with the successful movement to abolish child labour—and female labour in heavy industries like the mines —and continuing through the support for the establishment of free trade unions with the right to strike, for minimum wages and maximum working hours, the enforcement of minimum standards of health and safety in factories, and the like. Partly as a result of trade union pressure, partly as a result of a developing social conscience, partly through the political pressures of mass democracy, the industrial working environment has been enormously improved and humanised over the last century and a half.

Nevertheless, during the 1960s and early 1970s the pressures for change seemed to gather renewed force. On the one hand there have been strident and insistent demands that more should be done to fight pollution, to protect the environment from industrial despoliation, and to stop the alleged waste of non-renewable natural resources by forcing enterprises to 're-cycle' materials. Other demands have focused on the need to control the political powers of large enterprises, especially multinational companies which allegedly are able to evade control by the governments in whose territories they operate, and to make such companies more socially and politically responsible. Some would like to strengthen the power of consumers, others to make the control of business more democratic by insisting that representatives of the workers should sit on the boards of directors.

Another set of demands concerns the organisation of work itself. There are demands that workers should have greater security in their jobs than in the past; that there should be more democracy on the shopfloor, in the sense that workers should have more say in the organisation of their work; and that work itself should be 'enriched' or 'humanised', to do away with the monotonous drudgery of the assembly line, with its mindless routine.

We shall be looking at these issues, affecting the role of the business sector and the nature of work in the post-Keynesian economy, in more detail in Chapter 4. But two points need stressing here. First, these new demands being made on the industrial system represent, in a sense, simply a continuation and intensification of those being made in the nineteenth century. In the mid-nineteenth century people were beginning to argue that the survival of the capitalist system as a wealth-producing agency *ought not to require* as a necessary condition that women and young boys should pull coal-carts underground twelve hours a day and more; other, better means could be found to do the job. And so it proved. The capitalist system not only survived the loss of child labour. It flourished and developed.

Today we have reached the point at which people are beginning to argue that with our present technological knowledge it ought no longer to be necessary for men and women to submit, if they do not wish it, to the tyranny of the assembly line. In other words, our social consciences have become keener, *and so has our belief in the power of modern technology*. It is because we believe in the ability of technology, properly handled, to solve all problems that we feel justified in confronting it with demands which would have been thought utopian or irresponsible a decade or so ago.

This is the second point that needs to be made about the new demands on the system. There is, I believe, no accident about their timing. They reflect, partly, the spread of higher education. But, more fundamentally, they have emerged at a time when people had come to take for granted the continuation of full employment, economic growth, and the acceleration of technological advance. They came after two decades of almost continuous boom, when people had come to believe that the Keynesian system guaranteed an expanding economy. They came when the immediate needs of the mass of people in western society had been met, when

appetites had been whetted for further advances, when people felt
free to put more demands on the system in the belief that it was
indestructible (and, to be fair, when the adverse consequences and
risks of the prevailing pattern of economic growth were becoming
more evident).

The demands on the system have taken two forms: *material*
demands in the form of more ambitious wage claims; and *non-
material* demands of the kind discussed immediately above, to do
with the conduct and direction of the business sector, and the
nature of working conditions within it. Both sets of demands, I
have argued, possess a common origin in the inflation of expecta-
tion and the belief in the limitless powers of technology.

The Nemesis of Technology

I think we can now answer the question posed at the end of the
previous chapter. The ancient Greeks would have understood very
clearly what has been happening in the last decade. They would
see it as an example of *hubris* and *nemesis*, of the retribution
administered by Fate when men lost their natural humility and
ceased to fear the gods. Those forces which gave society its
stability—religion, the power of the State, the ignorance and
isolation of most individuals, the authority and stability of the
family—have been eroded, slowly at first and then increasingly
rapidly, by technological developments. Scientific discoveries
have discredited religious belief, and replaced it by materialism.
Rationality has replaced custom and authority. Communications
technology has replaced isolation with what the Canadian writer
Marshall McLuhan calls the 'global electronic village', and by
spreading knowledge of inequality has stimulated envy, ambition
and greed. Medical technology has opened the door to the
liberties and licence of the 'permissive society'. Finally, the balance
of power in society has been altered by the monopoly bargaining
power of trade unions, and perhaps even more by the fact that a
technologically complex society, such as ours has become, is
extremely dependent on the work of small groups of people, who
consequently acquire very great bargaining power.

These forces were building up at a time when men were beginning to believe that in the Keynesian system they had solved the problems of economic management, bringing what had previously been subject to autonomous and automatic forces under human management and control; and that in modern technology, which had solved so many hitherto insoluble problems and which had landed men on the moon, we had at our disposal an Aladdin's lamp which, given goodwill and competence, could bring wealth to all the globe.

Thus people came to believe that all things were possible—at a time when the curve of natural economic growth was almost certainly starting to level off. The demands being placed on the system were not, in isolation, unreasonable. Collectively they added up to far more than it could meet.

The situation can be expressed, crudely, by a mathematical equation. With present technology, the normal growth rate of the gross national product in all advanced industrial countries taken together, in times of buoyant market conditions, is around 5%–6% a year. Some countries, like Japan, fairly regularly exceed this rate—others, like the UK, very seldom attain it. But, as a world average, it represents about the best that can be achieved for other than very short periods of exceptional boom. The share of wages and salaries in the same countries hovers around 65% of total national income—or did, before the great inflation. This suggests that wage increases of much more than, say, 10% a year are going to be difficult to accommodate. A wage demand of 10%, over the western economies as a whole, can be offset as to one-half by increased output (as we have seen, given buoyant world trade). A shift in labour's share of the total national income of more than, say, 3%, at the expense of profits, tends to have very serious effects on industry's capacity to maintain its capital investment—and thus jeopardises the economic growth needed to pay future wage demands. Moreover, this 3% shift could only take place once—not year after year. (In fact, 3% is roughly the proportion by which labour has increased its share of national income in the western world as a whole during the great inflation.) A wage demand of 10% would therefore tend to lead, other things being equal, to a price increase of not less than 2%.

That, one might argue, is not too terrible; and indeed during the 1960s it was a not unusual pattern—wage increases somewhat ahead of output increases, with very fractional shifts in national income away from profits in favour of wages and salaries, and larger (but not dramatic) price rises. But what happens when wage increases accelerate from 10% a year to 20% or even 30%? The gap can only be filled by sharply increasing prices. This means that much of the original demand of the workers is frustrated, since the increased *money* wages they have gained do not produce the expected *real* increase in purchasing power. So they redouble their demands, in the hope that by anticipating the falling value of money they will be able to keep ahead of the spiral of prices and incomes; and in so doing, of course, they give the spiral a further twist.

This is indeed what happened in the period 1968–1974. Wage increases over the western world in these years averaged around 20%, and prices rose by more than 10% per annum (substantially more in certain countries such as the UK, Italy and Japan). Between 1962 and 1973 the share of profits in total national income fell by 3% in the UK (to 4.9%), by 2% in Japan (to 8.2%), by 1% in the US and Italy (to 6.9% and 2.8% respectively), and by rather under 1% in France (to 4.8%). The trend continued in 1974 and 1975, but comparable figures are not yet available. At the same time business was faced with the complex of non-material (but costly to implement) demands listed briefly in this chapter.

So, if we ask what it is that has gone wrong with the economic system during the last ten years, the answer I believe is that we have, individually and collectively, been demanding more from it than it is capable of delivering, at current levels of technology. The acceleration of wage demands has been a major element in this development, though by no means the only one. Nor is it reasonable to blame the inflation, as some do, on the excessive power or irresponsibility of the trade unions. The trade unions are

the most important institutional channels through which grievances are transmitted in our society. But the grievances themselves,
as I have suggested, have sprung from very deep changes in our
society and culture—changes which the unions could not have
ignored.

Just why this complex of pressures should have built up, at this
particular moment of history, I have tried in this and the last
chapter to explain. In the next two chapters I will try to analyse
some of the consequences.

3
Inflation and the State

If one ceases to believe in an after-life, if one agrees with
Nietzsche's Zarathustra that 'God is Dead', one becomes more
impatient to secure the good things of life in this existence—
especially if one is continually made aware of them by the mass
media, and if one has been taught to believe that with modern
technology all things are possible. Here we have what was perhaps the prime motivator of the great inflation of the last decade.

But there were other elements at work as well. One was the
enhanced social mobility which resulted from the great post-war
boom. In a number of occupations—notably in the worlds of
entertainment, sport, fashion, 'pop', property development, and
in certain sections of the service trades—there have been in all
western countries spectacular examples in the post-war years of
men and women from very humble backgrounds achieving very
great wealth. The demonstration effect of these 'rags-to-riches'
stories has been considerable, and it has reinforced the 'everything
is possible' attitude which characterised the late-1950s and the
1960s.

The younger generation in particular have tended to cut loose
from the tentacles of class background, and to see themselves as a
self-contained group outside the class system. They have been
united in their dislike of authority, whether it be the authority of
the university, the State, industrial bosses or trade union officials.

These are the attitudes which conditioned the inflationary
upsurge which brought the Keynesian era to an end. There is no
point at this stage in trying to form value judgements on them,
or on the new society towards which they point. Certain aspects
of the revolt against tradition are indeed extremely attractive.

The social disciplines described in the last chapter undoubtedly had their negative side. In too many cases they frustrated or stultified the human spirit, destroyed initiative and dreams, encouraged meanness, cruelty, intolerance and injustice. In return they gave security, both physically and spiritually.

The world of the 1960s, dizzy with economic success, had begun to feel that it no longer needed security, that it was time to achieve the full liberation of the human spirit. The tragedy is not that it was reaching out for new standards, but that it over-estimated the ability of the productive system to meet its demands.

The nations of the west, faced with new inflationary wage demands, sought without much success to contain them. A series of confrontations between governments and major unions revealed an alarming fact—that in present-day conditions democratic governments do not necessarily have the power, even if they have the will, to win a head-on confrontation with a powerful and determined trade union.

We saw in Chapter 1 how in 1968 the most powerful government in western Europe had to yield in a conflict with the weakest and most divided trade union movement of any European democracy. What happened in France then was repeated, if less dramatically, in other countries. In the USA the administration of President Nixon, which came to power in 1968 with a strong anti-inflation programme, reversed policy in 1970 in order to give priority to maintaining employment. In the UK the Conservative government of Mr Edward Heath fought two decisive battles against the National Union of Mineworkers, and lost on both occasions. In 1972 a wage increase of 21% was reluctantly conceded. At the end of 1973 the government was driven to impose a three-day week on industry in order to conserve coal stocks during a miners' overtime ban, and then to call a general election to give it the authority to deal with the miners. The election was lost, and the incoming Labour government gave the miners a further increase ranging from £6.71 to £16.31 a week in order to settle the dispute and get the country back to work.

Thus the verdict of the 1926 general strike was reversed nearly half-a-century later, and the miners succeeded in bringing down a Tory government which stood in their way. The triumph of the unions was the more complete in that they had successfully defeated attempts by both Labour and Conservative administrations to bring in legislation to control their activities. By 1974 the trade unions appeared all-powerful on the British political scene.

In other countries the change in the balance of power seemed less dramatic, but this was partly because few other governments were prepared to risk the head-on confrontations with union power which the British Conservatives undertook. When governments did try to resist excessive wage demands, or to support employers in so doing, they were more often defeated than successful. But in most cases they hardly tried.

This was the more remarkable, in that the years of runaway wage inflation were years of above-average unemployment, by post-war standards. The 'Phillips curve' ceased to have any apparent relevance after 1968. The unions were able to press their claims home in a weak labour market, largely because the tone was set by groups like the miners who were not affected by unemployment, and other bargainers tended to follow the trend set by the strong.

Social Appeasement and its Consequences

The effect of governments' capitulation to wages pressure was highly corrosive. For the first time since the end of the Middle Ages, governments in peacetime were seen to be unable to control sections of their subjects. More important, the ability of government to ensure social justice, to reward those who showed restraint, came into doubt; and with it a large part of the moral authority of democratically-elected administrations. Citizens showed increasing disrespect for, and disenchantment with, the forces of law and order. There was a growing tendency for groups and individuals throughout society to take matters into their own hands, and to take steps to ensure that whoever else suffered, they at least did not lose out in the struggle to keep up with inflation. There was a steady escalation of violence in society.

The loosening of social cohesion, the decline of respect and belief in the authority of the established institutions of society, is perhaps the most dangerous by-product of inflation. If the State could not protect its citizens from the ravages of inflation, why should they owe loyalty to it? Thomas Hobbes in *Leviathan*, writing at the time of the emergence of the modern nation-state in the mid-seventeenth century, argued that the authority of the monarch, his right to command unquestioning loyalty from his subjects, rested entirely on his ability to preserve them from the terrors of the life of nature, wherein man's life was 'nasty, brutish and short'. But if that ability was lost, why should men serve and obey the monarch? Every man has a right to self-preservation, and if that cannot be served by loyalty to the State and its laws, then the State has little right to expect loyalty or obedience.

In their reaction to inflationary pressures governments have been, and are, highly schizophrenic. On the one hand they have sought, not very successfully, to fight them. On the other hand they have felt obliged to compensate the victims of inflation—the pensioners, those on fixed incomes, workers whose bargaining power is weak—and by increasing their incomes in line with rising prices, they have of course given an added twist to the inflationary spiral. One can appreciate governments' dilemma in not wanting the innocent to suffer as a result of the failure of others to control inflation. But the connivance of governments in inflation has in fact gone further than this. The monetarists are at least partly right. Governments have shared, at least to some extent, in the fever that struck the peoples of the west in the 1960s, the 'revolution of rising expectations'.

All western countries have developed, since 1945, expensive and comprehensive welfare state systems. In every western country the State subsidises education, housing, health provision, and provides special assistance to those with large families or with very low incomes. In every country the State provides pensions for the old, widows, the unemployed, the injured and chronically sick. State spending on social protection in all forms has grown steadily throughout the Keynesian era, as a major part of the dividend from national economic growth. But from the mid-1960s on-wards the rate of public welfare spending has tended to accelerate in relation to the growth of industrial production in the great majority of western countries.

A number of reasons can be advanced for this phenomenon. The massive growth in higher education, which was seen as a long-term investment in economic development, was one factor. Another was the belief, which governments shared with their subjects, that economic growth could be relied on to continue indefinitely, and it was therefore important to see that the fruits of growth were more equitably distributed—and how could this be better done than through the transfer mechanisms and social investment of the State?

A third factor was the way in which the growing public sector has come to be organised in all western countries. Everywhere one sees a similar pattern. Powerful government departments have grown up, with ministers sitting in Cabinet, with a vested interest in securing a bigger share of the national 'cake' to finance their ambitious long-term spending programmes. Behind and below them are the organisations of those concerned with the pro-grammes—the doctors, teachers, nurses, health service workers, local government officials, and the like—whose livelihoods and career prospects depend on the maintenance and expansion of the programmes. Increasingly these groups of workers have come to organise themselves in powerful and effective trade unions. There is thus an increasingly strong and well-organised lobby for the expansion of each one of the public welfare services. None of the services is subject to the disciplines of the market economy, since they are not freely traded on the open market. Their size and direction depends on governmental decisions. No government, to my knowledge, has yet been able to devise a system for the objective definition of criteria which will determine the right share of public services in the total national income, and the right priorities within the overall total of public spending. Both the total size, and the share-out within the total, tend to be settled in annual discussions within the Cabinet, and to depend much more on the political power of the individual ministers concerned than on any clearly-defined objective criteria. But there is a strong in-built tendency for the total figure to increase as a share of national income.

This is particularly true at a time of high inflation—for two reasons. By and large, the public services sector is highly labour-intensive. This means that its costs rise more than proportionally when wages and salaries rise. This helps to explain why, over the last decade, the costs of public services have risen steeply despite a general decline in their quality; the public authorities have tried to find ways of economising to offset increased staff costs, and the result has left everybody dissatisfied.

The second reason is that a substantial part of the services provided by the welfare state are designed to compensate the poor for a worsening in their plight. Wage inflation, as we have seen, leaves some people greatly worse off—pensioners, those on fixed incomes, the unemployed, those with very low incomes and weak bargaining power. Inflation redistributes income in an arbitrary and unfair way. A major purpose of the welfare state is to protect the sufferers, and to restore an element of social justice through what is called the 'social wage'. Thus inflation puts extra demands on the State purse.

Leviathan Expands—Capitalism Contracts

So throughout the great inflation the share of public spending in total national income has been growing—in some countries at an alarming speed. In the UK, for example, it grew from 40% to over 60% (on certain definitions), between 1961 and 1975. How did governments finance this increase? Only part of it was paid for by raising taxes. A large part was financed by borrowing, by increasing government debt. To this extent the monetarist thesis is true. In order to maintain their own programmes of public spending in an era of rapidly rising costs, and to adapt them to the new requirements arising from inflation, governments allowed the money supply to increase at a rate which without doubt added further fuel to the inflationary flames.[1]

It would be wrong, however, to give the impression that the whole of the increase in the share of national income going to public spending has been due to welfare payments. There is another element, which has been particularly important in the weaker countries in the western world, notably Italy and the UK. The era of inflation has seen a substantial increase in the State's share of the productive system.

This has not happened as a result of a planned strategy for the extension of nationalisation or public enterprise. It has happened because governments have sought to halt or slow down the inflationary spiral at the politically easiest point, by trying to stop firms from passing on cost increases in the form of higher prices. In the case of the nationalised industries this has meant that government has had to provide massive subsidies to cover deficits incurred in the furtherance of anti-inflation policy. In paying these subsidies government has in many cases had to borrow money itself, with inflationary effects on the money supply.

In the case of the private sector, the effect has been to reduce very sharply the profit margins on which firms operate, and thus to make it much harder for them to finance further capital investment or to attract money from the private capital market (the Stock Exchange or the banks). It is no accident that the inflationary era produced a massive slump in share prices and unprecedentedly high rates of interest (in money though not in real terms). So, particularly in Great Britain and Italy—but also in Germany and some other countries—the early 1970s saw some spectacular bankruptcies and near-bankruptcies in the private sector. To be fair, by no means all of these were due to government price controls. A more important cause was either sheer management miscalculation, or the lethal effect of long-term fixed-price contracts which did not allow for the escalation of costs during the contract (particularly important for heavy capital goods firms like shipbuilders for example). In any event, government was faced with the prospect of either allowing major enterprises to go bankrupt, with consequent heavy unemployment and loss of export business, or replacing private finance by government money.

In most cases government preferred to take the latter course, with the result that there was a substantial migration of weak firms from the private sector to the public sector, where they were no longer subject to the constraints of the market economy in financing future development. In the UK firms which took this route during the early 1970s included household names like Rolls Royce, British Leyland, Ferranti, Alfred Herbert, Harland & Wolff, and the British operations of Chrysler. Other industries nominally in the private sector, like shipbuilding and aircraft manufacture (both nationalised in 1977), rely heavily on government for finance. So government has become a substantial provider of manufacturing finance, which again has increased its need to borrow.

So, for a variety of reasons, over the inflationary period government spending has seemed to be increasingly out of control, pre-empting a larger and larger share of national resources in every western country; with practically every government spending well beyond its means and thus getting deeper and deeper into debt, disbursing IOUs which serve to inflate the money supply and to divert scarce capital from the productive sector of the economy.

These problems were severe enough up to 1973, but in that year things took a sharp turn for the worse. The oil-exporting countries, organised together in OPEC, collectively decided to increase the cost of their oil fourfold. This must be the most dramatic example of successful cartel action in the history of the world, and as an exercise in 'cost-push' inflation it knocked the last nail into the coffin of the Keynesian boom. It produced, almost overnight, a massive switch in the balance of world economic and purchasing power. The oil-producing countries acquired an enormous balance of payments surplus, both with the western industrial countries and with the non-oil-producing developing countries. The western world went heavily into debt, and had to divert a substantial part of national production into increased exports to pay for the oil it needed to keep its economies going. While the USA, potentially self-sufficient in energy, could absorb the shock, the impact on western Europe, Japan and developing countries like Brazil and the Indian sub-continent was very severe (though the UK expects to achieve self-sufficiency in energy through the exploitation of North Sea deposits by 1980).

The most immediate result of the OPEC action was to precipitate the most severe recession which the west had experienced since the 1930s. It is probable that the cumulative imbalances generated by the inflation—notably the draining of resources out of the private and into the public sector which we have just described—would sooner or later have pushed the world into a recession. But the oil price rise at the very least accelerated and intensified the process. During 1974 and 1975 unemployment rates throughout the advanced industrial countries approximately doubled, increasing in the nine countries of the European Economic Community (EEC) from $2\frac{1}{2}\%$ to over 5%, or upwards of 5 million people out of a 100-million work-force. The western world was confronted with the hitherto almost unknown phenomenon of 'stagflation'—inflation accompanied by economic decline and high unemployment—a combination regarded as impossible according to orthodox Keynesian economics.

The slump certainly had some impact on inflation—which, after the sharp extra twist given by the leap in oil prices, levelled off and began to show some signs of decline in 1976. The fall-off was sharpest in West Germany, the USA and Switzerland (and, for quite different reasons, in Mrs Gandhi's India). But it remained well into double figures in the UK, Italy, Ireland and France, while increasing in previously stable Sweden. The disparity in inflation rates during 1976 has caused major problems of economic integration within the EEC, where the rich countries get richer and the poor poorer almost week by week.

The End of Full Employment

But, whereas there is great diversity in inflation rates, unemployment levels show a certain similarity throughout the EEC. The great boom of the Keynesian era did not produce uniformly-spread full employment. There were, and are, marked regional disparities, with unemployment rates remaining obstinately high in the remoter regions—southern Italy, Ireland and the northern and western parts of the UK. At the same time the central areas of the Community were sucking in very large numbers of migrant workers, both from other parts of the Community and from countries outside (Turkey, Greece, Yugoslavia, Spain, Portugal, North Africa and, in the UK, immigrants from the Indian sub-continent and the Caribbean). In 1975 it was estimated that there were approximately 12 million migrants with their dependents living in the EEC countries, of whom one-third came from other Community member-states and two-thirds from the third world. The great *Völkerwanderung* into the booming industrial heartlands of western Europe during the Keynesian era—one of the largest over a comparable time-span in recorded history—owed much, of course, to the development of modern means of mass trans-portation: another instance of the unlooked-for side-effects of technology on society.

For the unevenness of economic development, and the centri-petal forces of economic integration, has been one of the main criticisms mounted against the pursuit of economic growth since the war. It is clear that corrective forces have to be applied, to spread economic activity more evenly geographically. We shall be discussing some of the implications of this in Chapter 6. At this point, however, it is necessary to stress the specific problems posed by the migration from the Mediterranean countries in the EEC—problems which have changed radically in their nature since 1974.

The problems of migration up to 1974 in the EEC were essenti-ally those of social integration. There was no doubt that the EEC needed the labour, or that the Mediterranean countries had a sur-plus available. The problem was rather that the host countries could not, or would not, take the necessary steps to see that the migrants and their families had reasonable access to the benefits to which, by paying taxes, they contributed—to housing, schooling for their children, social security, medical and other welfare ser-vices. They were tending to concentrate in urban ghettos in the decaying centres of Europe's big industrial cities, a sub-proletariat without rights or roots in the communities which were exploiting their labour while denying them social equality. In short, their situation was becoming alarmingly like that of the blacks and Spanish Americans in the big cities of the US—an alien, embittered, undigested minority of poor people performing the jobs which the indigenous peoples around them disdain.

These problems remain, but since 1974 they have been overtaken by a new situation. Faced with recession and mounting unemployment at home, each of the big EEC labour-importing countries—Germany, France, the Benelux countries—has stopped accepting migrants from outside the Community (within the EEC there is of course free movement of labour, so there is no way in which Italians, for example, can be prevented from entering Germany or France to seek jobs). Outside the Continental EEC, Switzerland has adopted a similar policy, while in the UK and Scandinavia controls on immigration, always strict, have been tightened (there are exceptions for Commonwealth citizens in the UK, while there is free movement of labour within the Scandinavian bloc). At the same time migrants working in the EEC and Switzerland on fixed-term contracts are being forced to return home as their contracts expire, so that the proportion of third-country migrants in the total labour force in these countries is declining.

This process has very important, and disquieting, consequences for the group of Mediterranean countries which over the years have come to rely on the EEC as an outlet for their surplus labour, and on the migrants' remittances as a support for their balances of payments. None of them (with the possible exception of Greece) has a strong enough economy to absorb anything like all the existing labour force, let alone a reflux of migrants. In each of them there is a very delicate social and political balance, resting on extremely fragile economies. All except Yugoslavia are either aspirant EEC members or have treaties of association with it; in Yugoslavia's case it must be a western European interest to strengthen links, so that the country will not be sucked back into the Soviet orbit after the death of President Tito.

All this would argue for a liberal policy of immigration on the part of the EEC. But unfortunately the prognosis on unemployment in western Europe is extremely depressing. All the forecasts suggest that there will be substantial unemployment at least up to 1980 and probably beyond. So the ability, and the willingness, of the EEC countries to start absorbing again large numbers of workers from third countries is going to be strictly limited for some time to come.

The EEC therefore has to develop, as rapidly as possible, a strategy for dealing with the problems of the outpost of the impoverished third world on its southern doorstep. It cannot continue indefinitely to ban all immigration, for that is a 'beggar-my-neighbour' policy of exporting unemployment to countries much less capable of coping with it than the EEC itself. On the other hand it can hardly afford to re-open the floodgates and revert to the pre-1974 free-for-all. So there has to be, on the one hand, a Community-wide controlled immigration policy, relating the influx of workers to the jobs available and to the capacity of the host communities to provide a reasonable social infrastructure— and on the other hand, as soon as circumstances permit, a generous programme of capital development, to create jobs in the countries whence the migrants come (just as the Regional and Social Fund and the European Investment Bank help to provide jobs in the remoter regions of the Community itself).

The migrants form one particular aspect of Europe's labour market problem; the areas of regional deprivation another. There are two other sections of the community for whom the recession has been especially traumatic—and in each case the causes and the consequences extend well beyond the labour market into other aspects of modern society. These two groups are *women* and the *young* (girls and boys).

Women and Children Last?

Among the under-privileged groups in the labour market before 1974, women figured prominently. In many—perhaps most— jobs, women were paid less than men doing equivalent work.

They had fewer opportunities for training and promotion. Girls' schools tended to prepare women either for marriage, or for a limited number of jobs regarded as peculiarly suitable for females (and usually badly paid in consequence).

The reasons for this discrimination are fairly obvious. The traditional role of women in western society has been that of wife, mother and housekeeper. A large number of working women are girls who are expected to leave work once they start a family, or housewives supplementing the family income (often working part-time); the full-time career woman has been regarded as something of an oddity until relatively recently. Perhaps because they saw working life as only a phase in their career, perhaps because they were not normally the main family breadwinner, women have tended to be much less interested in joining trade unions and much less militant in pressing for better pay and conditions than men. Also, entry by women into certain jobs has been prohibited by law (it is illegal in many countries for women to work on night shift, for example)—and in many other cases by trade union restrictions.

Since the war, however, women have become increasingly restive in face of these discriminations. The proportion of women in the total work-force has risen steadily, so that they now account for one in every three west European workers. They are found particularly in two groups of industries—in low-paid retail or manufacturing jobs (especially clothing and textiles) or nursing; and at the other end of the scale, in the fast-growing sector of 'tertiary' services (government, secretarial services, education, leisure, etc.). But their share of the top jobs even in these sectors is still disproportionately small.

The reasons for women's increasing interest in jobs are not far to seek. As mechanisation replaces manual labour in industry after industry, the female skills of dexterity as opposed to male strength become more prized. Girls have benefited more than boys from the spread of higher education, if only because they started from further behind. Life as a housewife does not seem very challenging to the highly-educated girl. Housework has in any case become highly mechanised, so that on the one hand it requires less time, while on the other hand the capital equipment now available in the home is costly; why not take a job to pay for the mechanisation of one's home, rather than do the housework in the traditional way, by hand?

Other factors have contributed also. On the one hand, contraception enables married women to plan their families so that child-bearing will not interfere with a career. On the other, the greater ease and frequency of divorce within the 'permissive society' mean that the housewife without a job or a career has lost much of her traditional security; she cannot be certain, as she usually could in the past, that whatever other problems she or he may have, her man will provide for her. And, above all, women are questioning their traditional role in society, as wives and mothers in a structure of nuclear families. The 'revolution of women' is part cause, part consequence, of the challenge to the family which has emerged in modern western society.

The question of the future of the family must be reserved until later in this book. But what is clear is that the demands of women for a better deal at work, for greater participation in the economic wealth-creating structure, have to be accommodated. But it is also unhappily clear that these demands, like others we have noted already, have come at precisely the time when the industrial system can least afford to meet them. Specifically, when more women seek jobs in a period of recession and under-employment like the present, more women *and men* will join the dole-queue; and that is what is happening.

More important than women's unemployment, however, is the very sharp rise in those out of work in the under-25 age group (both boys and girls). One of the most alarming aspects of the 1974–76 recession has been the extent to which loss of jobs has been concentrated on this generation, in every country in the western world. The reasons are not far to seek. First, most employers practice—with the approval of the trade unions—'last-in-first-out' redundancy policies. When jobs are lost, it is therefore those with the least seniority, who will normally be the youngest, who will be the first to go. Second, as already indicated there is now more competition for jobs in this age-group between the sexes; the girls are challenging the boys for the available jobs to a much greater extent than ever before.

A third factor is that young labour is no longer, as in the past, cheap labour. Government legislation and trade union bargaining pressure have combined to raise the cost of young workers to equality, or near-equality, with that of fully-trained mature workers (if one takes into account the cost to the employer, in terms of cash and lost man-hours, of training). Moreover, the same forces have so raised the cost to the employer of dismissing a worker—especially a worker with long service—that labour is becoming much more of a fixed, and less of a variable, cost in the calculations of employers. This means that enterprises are becoming increasingly chary of taking on new workers, unless they are certain that they cannot meet orders without them, and that fluctuations in demand will not oblige them to get rid of them in the foreseeable future.

All these factors work against the young entrant to the labour market. But there is more. All the evidence suggests that in virtually every western country there is a growing mismatch, a failure of communication and understanding, between the educational world and the world of work. In every western country large numbers of young people are emerging from the—hugely enlarged—educational system with excellent qualifications, but with attitudes, or lack of certain essential aptitudes, which make them unattractive as employees to the business world.

Thus many students, particularly those who went through the centres of higher learning during the world-wide wave of student unrest in the late 1960s, regard the whole wealth-producing system with great suspicion—as a bastion of capitalistic privilege, a polluter of the environment, and so forth. Not surprisingly this hostile attitude is reciprocated by potential employers. Other students, not necessarily left-wing in their political beliefs, have come to favour a 'hippy' life-style which does not accord easily with the regimented style of the industrial world. Others again have been led to believe that their educational qualifications entitle them to a higher salary and a better job than the business world is prepared—given their lack of practical experience—to offer. And there are many others who suffer from lack of vocational guidance, that is to say of advice as to the kind of jobs which are available and which would satisfy them; thus they spend a substantial time moving from one job to another in search of their ideal, and in the process acquire a record which indicates fickleness and unreliability, so that eventually they run the risk of being classified by impatient employers as unemployables.

It is pointless to try to apportion blame for this very serious wastage of talent among the young in our advanced industrial democracies. What is clear is that there is an urgent need for more co-operation between the sellers (the educational world) and the customers (the business world). The latter need to specify much more clearly what they want, and to be more flexible and understanding in their handling of the product. Too often the business world continues to operate rigid hierarchical command structures which have gone out of fashion in the rest of society. But the educational authorities themselves need to understand that they live in, and are financed by, an industrial society, and that if they try to ignore this fact and fail to communicate with their main customer, the probability is that they too will find themselves redundant before long.

However, improvements in education-business liaison, badly needed as they are, will not solve the problems of youthful unemployment at a time of overall labour surplus. The indications are, as already stated, that this labour surplus will persist, even allowing for no further immigration, in western Europe into the 1980s. It needs little imagination to envisage the risks to society—as well as the personal tragedy and waste—of a generation of youths who move straight from school to the dole queue, and who after a few years may become embittered and unemployable. It is after all this generation which in Northern Ireland, on both sides of the religious divide, has found its only fulfilment in murder, intimidation and mindless violence; and in the early 1930s it was from the same ranks that Hitler drew the gangs of street-fighters and small-time bullies with which he destroyed the Weimar republic.

What Future for the Welfare State?

It seems therefore that, in the post-Keynesian era, government has to face two new, major challenges. The first concerns public expenditure on welfare services; the second the reconciliation of full employment with relatively low economic growth. As to the first, all governments accepted, in the immediate post-war era, a commitment to various kinds of social protection for their citizens. These commitments have grown, haphazardly, as part of the dividend from economic growth. During the inflationary period, as we have seen, they expanded much faster than economic growth, taking a larger and larger share of national resources. Now economic growth has slowed down dramatically, the problem has become more acute. Few western countries are in a position today to afford the full range of social expenditures to which successive governments have committed them.

What is to be done? It would be unthinkable for the west to turn its back on the welfare state concept. Inflation, as we have seen, increases the need for protection for those who cannot deploy economic strength; and when inflation is accompanied by unemployment, this is doubly true. Moreover, as we shall see in Chapter 8, a policy of social protection and reform is an integral part of an anti-inflation strategy based on agreement with the trade unions. But at the same time, the State cannot go on as it has been doing, especially in countries like the UK and Italy, with weak economic structures, paying welfare cheques which it cannot strictly honour, pre-empting resources which are needed for capital investment in the productive sector or for exports.

The solution therefore must lie in much more careful planning by the State in the social sphere. There has to be a clear assessment of the country's social needs and priorities, and of the resources available to meet them. There has to be agreement on the proportion of the national income which can properly be used for social

expenditure, as against consumer spending, private capital investment, exports and other public spending (e.g. defence, repayment
of foreign debt, etc.). There has to be an informed debate on the
proper role of the State in meeting social needs, and of the changing social requirements of a population which is itself changing
rapidly in demographic terms, in standards of living and in
aspirations.

Hitherto such debate as has taken place has tended to be at the
margins of social spending. Should we give priority next year to
building schools or council houses? Should hospitals take priority
over roads—subsidising school meals over raising old age pensions
—primary schools over universities—and so on? Much even of
this debate takes place in private, between the big spending departments of State and the Treasury. There is little attempt to find out
the priorities of the public, either directly by means of referenda
or questionnaires (though the techniques of opinion sampling are
well developed, and much used on issues of considerably less importance), or through consultation with consumers' representatives
such as the trade unions and other public bodies. (There is however a good deal of consultation with the *producer* representatives
—the unions, professional groups or other lobbies whose interest
lies in promoting one or other form of public spending).

It would certainly be desirable to open up this debate on the
future guidelines for social spending to a wider audience, within
the context of the kind of 'social contract' to be discussed in
Chapter 8. But will this go far enough? I fear that we have gone
beyond the stage when we have to examine marginal changes and
re-timings of expenditures in a steadily expanding total budget.
The dilemma facing governments today is to decide where real
and continuing cuts of substantial magnitude can be made in
public social spending—cuts which must almost certainly lead,
sooner or later, to the State withdrawing altogether from certain
fields where it is currently the paymaster.

This kind of debate has hardly yet started in any western country—though there are in many countries political parties which
are prepared to challenge the whole basis of the Welfare State,

and which have tended to gain strength very rapidly during the mid-1970s.

One element in the debate is how far we should subsidise institutions, and how far individuals. Much of the attack on the State welfare system has focused on the extent to which it has created large, unwieldy, unrepresentative, self-perpetuating institutions. The apparatus of transfer payments, whereby money is transferred via the State from one citizen to another, is criticised as bureaucratic, labour-intensive, and often regressive in its results. The poor who have not been lucky enough to find council houses subsidise the poor—or the not-so-poor—who have. Workers on low incomes would often be better off not working, and drawing social security. That is one line of attack. Another is that in creating social welfare institutions the State is frustrating its own objectives. A large part of the money designed to help relieve sickness goes on the administration of hospitals. Too much of the education budget goes, not to the increase of learning and wisdom among the people, but to the establishment and maintenance of a large and costly infrastructure of schools, technical colleges and universities. To the demand for more cost-effective methods of increasing welfare in the community is added the distrust, characteristic of the 1970s, of all large institutions, whether they be in the public or the private sector.

This new populism has to be taken into account by government in assessing the priorities for public spending, and the means by which it can be effected. There is a growing demand for wider participation in the debate on the future of the Welfare State. There is a growing urgency in demands for examination of systems of tax credits to individuals to replace some of the earmarked grants to specific institutions. Thus it has been argued that freedom of parental choice can be combined with a publicly-financed education system by giving people tax credits cashable at a range of schools, rather than directing all pupils to specific schools. This would not only give individuals more choice in a vital sector, but it would also reintroduce into part of the non-market sector some of the disciplines and incentives of the competitive market system.

Similarly, it has been argued that much of the bureaucratic complexity of individual benefits and disbenefits could be abolished by the introduction of a 'negative income tax' system, whereby each citizen would receive tax credits for his welfare entitlements, which would be offset against his tax payments. Some would end up as net taxpayers, others as net tax receivers. The individual would receive much more of his welfare benefit than today in cash rather than in kind, giving him or her a greater latitude in the way in which it was spent. The government would be able to influence income distribution much more effectively and less haphazardly than today.

The technical difficulties of such a move should not be under-estimated, though the development of computer techniques has made them much less overwhelming than even a few years ago. But it seems clear, whatever one's political beliefs, that the Welfare State system, which grew up alongside and in the shadow of the Keynesian world order, has reached a dead end. It no longer satisfies anyone, it no longer provides value for money, it no longer directs resources into the areas defined as being of greatest need. In short, a major re-thinking is needed. But first, government needs to reorganise itself so that this debate can be meaningfully undertaken.

The Employment Dilemma

Unfortunately, with the recession a major new preoccupation has arisen in the area of public spending, which—other things equal—must greatly *increase* social spending, and will do so for some years to come. Just as governments in the post-war heyday undertook commitments in the field of *social protection* (in the UK with the wartime Beveridge report, implemented by the post-war Labour government), so at the same time they accepted explicit commitments to *full employment* (in the UK this was formally done in 1944). Just as the Welfare State was regarded as a kind of dividend from economic growth, whose parameters did not require major examination so long as that growth continued, so full employment was assumed to be a function of effective Keynesian policies of demand management, at the macro-economic level. As we saw in Chapter 1, the great Keynesian discovery was that governments, by successful manipulation of the various elements of demand, could and should maintain economic activity at a level which would ensure full employment and the maintenance of economic growth and stability.

But what happens when the commitments to full employment and to economic viability are in conflict? This is the new situation which has emerged in the 1970s. The scenarios for the next five years suggest that it will not be possible in most western countries to carry through macro-economic policies which would ensure a return to full employment, without recreating the inflationary pressures which came near to wrecking the western socio-economic system in the last five.

It is impossible to say whether the downturn in inflation which has taken place since 1975 is a lasting phenomenon or a temporary breathing-space. The optimists say that the inflation was a temporary fever, a malfunctioning of society, and that now we have come to recognise its evil and self-defeating nature we will be able to avoid it in future. The pessimists reply that the virus which caused the fever is still at large, that the biggest post-war recession has failed to restore conditions to normal (though it has certainly contributed to a reduction of the fever), and that as and when the world economy returns to a higher level of activity a recrudescence of inflation is to be feared.

Clearly this is a question vital to the future of our society, and while the answer remains in doubt governments are going to err on the side of caution in reflating their economies—especially those who, like the West Germans, have traumatic folk-memories of the havoc wreaked by runaway inflation after both world wars. That is one reason why macro-economic policies are unlikely, by themselves, to restore full employment over the next few years.

It is not, however, the only one. We have already seen that the cost to an employer of laying off workers—and in some cases the political difficulty of so doing—has made labour more of a fixed than a variable cost, and has made employers more reluctant, at any level of economic activity, to take on new workers. Furthermore, recent advances in technology—especially in the field of automation—have greatly increased potential output per worker. During the recession these technical advances have continued, but actual productivity has fallen, because of the cost and difficulty for an employer of reducing his labour force. This means that there is an exceptionally large amount of 'slack' in the western economies, in the form of under-employed workers. So the revival in demand will have to go a long way before there is much erosion of the numbers out of work.

Another reason why unemployment levels are likely to stay high is simply that over the next few years there will be more people of working age in our society, as a result of the boom in the birth rate during the optimistic and expanding 1950s. With the growth rate in manufacturing and primary industry levelling off, and the underlying rate of productivity steadily increasing—as a result of higher levels of technology and the progressive introduction of automation—the industrial world has been moving since the mid-1960s into a structural imbalance between the demand and supply of labour. There is no sign that this will do anything other than intensify for the rest of this decade, for there has been no change in the factors behind it. Some of the manpower released from the manufacturing sector has been absorbed by the expanding services sector—but not enough; and the cutback in *public* services, which we have seen in preceding pages to be necessary, will worsen this aspect of the situation. Some of the gain from extra productivity has been absorbed by longer holidays and reduced working hours, but not enough to leave the demand for labour intact. There simply has not been enough investment in new activities to take up the slack brought about by stagnation in the manufacturing sector. Nor, given the depressed rate of investment throughout the industrialised world, is there any sign that enough will be forthcoming over the next few years to mop up the structurally unemployed.

Finally, there is the fact that present welfare state systems, coupled with high rates of personal tax, constitute a disincentive for certain groups of people to take jobs—particularly if the only work available is dirty, unpleasant or dangerous, or if it involves moving from one's home. It may be more attractive or advantageous to draw unemployment benefit.

For the first time, therefore, governments are going to have to consider full employment as an objective apart from overall Keynesian demand management. This is going to take us into some strange and difficult areas. For example, rather than compensate people for unemployment should we not rather subsidise employment? Instead of using tax incentives to promote capital investment, should we not rather encourage firms to develop labour-intensive techniques—even though according to conventional thinking this is a step backwards technologically? How far can or should government go in deliberate *job creation*, by providing employment in public works projects or in community developments for people who would otherwise be without work? How far should *work sharing* be promoted—by, for example, radically reducing the working week and/or lowering the retirement age, in order deliberately to create more job vacancies for unemployed young people? How far can or should one go in encouraging firms to vary the working pattern, by introducing flexible working hours ('flexitime'), and by encouraging employees to take 'sabbaticals' in mid-career, to re-train or re-educate themselves, and incidentally provide a temporary job opportunity for somebody else?

There are strong arguments against any one of these measures. Without exception they would be costly—increasing public spending at a time when all the evidence suggests it should be cut —and they would lower productivity (at least by conventional accounting standards), at a time when all western economies are competing against each other in keenly contested world markets. A country would need to avoid jeopardising jobs in competitive sectors as the price of promoting jobs elsewhere. Moreover, if the advanced western economies are encouraged to turn their back on capital-intensive technology in favour of more traditional labour-intensive technology, how will they be able to compete against the newly-industrialising countries whose labour costs are much lower than theirs? Should they not be abandoning this area to those who can cover it better, and concentrate instead on the high-technology industries where they still have an advantage? Finally, early retirement, if carried too far, could simply mean transferring the burden of unemployment from one group of workers (the young) to another group (the elderly), who are in fact more productive and better motivated.

One of the difficulties is that the unemployed, as such, have no trade union. While they are sensitive to the rate of unemployment and the problems of the unemployed, the trade unions must in practice give priority to protecting the interests of their members in work—who, after all, pay the dues which keep the unions in business.

It will not, therefore, be easy to promote employment for social reasons, or to find adequate outlets for labour-intensive technology. Employment-creation measures will be more effective if they are undertaken in concert by a group of countries, rather than by a single country acting in isolation, which would be vulnerable to competition in world markets. The development of labour-intensive technology should take place in areas outside the traditional low-cost, labour-intensive manufacturing industries, which the advanced countries should be ceding to the developing countries in the interests of a new world economic order (see Chapter 6 below). That this can be done will be seen in the next chapter, when we look at work-humanisation methods in Scandinavia and elsewhere. There is also scope for labour-intensive technology in services and in non-export industries (bread and beer are good examples)—especially where such techniques can reduce the cost of other high-cost inputs such as energy. So there is room for more emphasis on the introduction of labour-intensive investment even in the advanced industrial countries; but the opportunities need to be carefully defined.

Moreover, we need to avoid a 'spill-over' from the secondary labour market of publicly-financed community jobs, to the primary labour market financed by the market economy. The two markets need to be kept totally distinct, so that subsidised secondary labour market operators cannot compete for contracts with operators in the primary labour market—and employers cannot replace normal workers with State-subsidised workers. (Otherwise of course the trade unions will kill job-creation schemes.) Finally, we are going to have to soften and blur the rigid line which has been maintained between work and leisure (or education, or training, or retirement) in capitalist society. 'Work' will increasingly be a good to be shared rather than an obligation to be undertaken. One might indeed envisage a threefold division of the national work-force between the fully-employed, the unemployed, and the 'socially-employed': the last category working, either whole- or part-time, in socially useful but non-profit-earning activities (of which the US Peace Corps, and UK equivalents such as Voluntary Service Overseas—VSO—and Community Service Volunteers—CSV—would be examples). Those employed in this third sector would expect a low standard of living, but, one hopes, an above-average standard of job satisfaction.

It will take time, however, to evolve the new structures and the new thinking which will be required to give effect to these changes. And in the meantime governments face a conflicting set of objectives. On the one hand they have to establish macro-economic strategies which will enable sufficient resources to go into exports and into productive capital investment, to restore the balance of payments and to get their economies once more on to a growth path. This requires a curb on public spending and a continuing restraint on consumer spending. As far as the latter is concerned, there have been periods in recent years when people reacted to the decline in purchasing power—as they have historically done in earlier inflations—by running down their savings and buying goods instead. Surprisingly, however, this tendency has declined in the mid-1970s, and savings have remained very high in most western countries despite the continuing fall in money values. Since prices have been rising faster than incomes during the recession—in most, though not all, western countries—real disposable spending power has declined. But for how long will the trade unions allow this to continue?

So governments have to improve the allocation of resources within their economies in order to promote growth and efficiency. At the same time they have to take steps to counter the menace of structural unemployment, steps which at first glance seem to run directly counter to this primary objective. The connecting link, and a possible reconciliation between the two objectives, I suggest, will be found by establishing a viable policy to deal with the basic problem underlying both phenomena—the depression and the unemployment: the problem of inflation.

We shall return to this central theme in Chapter 7. In the meantime, however, we need to examine what inflation and its accompanying phenomena have done to the business enterprise, and to society at large. These questions will occupy the next three chapters.

NOTE TO CHAPTER 3

[1] Some people argue that the expansion in public spending was simply correcting a previous imbalance in western economies, which were devoting too much of their resources to consumer spending in the private sector, too little to public welfare. Thus western society was characterised during the Keynesian boom by the coexistence of private affluence and public squalor. This thesis was advanced with considerable force, eloquence and wit by the American economist J. K. Galbraith in *The Affluent Society* at the end of the 1950s. Certainly the rise in public sector spending was, in part at least, a response to real demands. But, because public and private consumer goods are traded in separate 'markets', as it were—so that the individual never has the ability to choose between, for example, buying a new car or, by increasing his taxes, improving the road system—it is extremely difficult at any point to argue conclusively that any society is spending 'too much' or 'too little' on public welfare. The recognition of the essential difference between the 'economic' and the 'political' market has led two such distinguished American economists as Galbraith and Milton Friedman (see below, Chapter 7) to diametrically opposite policy conclusions.

4

Inflation and the Firm

In the Keynesian economic order, as in the classical economic order which preceded it, the role of the business sector was clearly defined. The main economic objective of governments was *growth*—the fastest rate of growth consistent with economic stability. For the achievement of this objective, governments depended on the performance of the business sector. Thus government had an inescapable concern with business performance, and therefore with the best allocation of resources between enterprises. The performance of enterprises was measured by *profits*, and it was relative profits which determined the movement of resources within the productive system. Profits measured efficiency, and it was through differences in profit margins that resources were induced to flow out of the less efficient and into the more efficient sectors of the economy. The relationship between enterprises was established by *competition*, and it was the existence of competition which ensured that relative profits truly reflected relative efficiency in performance. At the macro level, the relationship between the business sector as a whole and the other major elements in society was regulated by what the American economist Kenneth Galbraith christened '*countervailing power*'—the tendency for workers, consumers and other sections to group together to resist domination by the business community.

This syndrome—growth / profits / competition / countervailing power—was not of course always achieved, nor were its results always perfect. But it constituted a norm towards which the capitalist economy was always aiming, and in so far as it was achieved it ensured a balance of forces within society, in which the role of each sector was clear and understood. In particular it identified a role for the enterprise and a standard against which its performance could be clearly measured, given competitive conditions and a free market.

This balance has hardly survived the post-Keynesian inflation. Countervailing power, as we have seen, has been unbalanced by the dominating position achieved by the trade unions and professional pressure groups, which has created a chronic bias towards *cost inflation*. Governments have tried to prevent firms from passing on cost increases, with the result that more and more enterprises are moving from a position of profit to one of relying on government *subsidy*. When governments move into the productive sector, they have a natural tendency to seek to replace competition in that sector by *monopoly*. Finally, during the post-Keynesian era growth has first of all been challenged as a reasonable economic objective on the part of government (I shall be discussing the 'growth debate' in Chapter 7), and more recently has disappeared, to be replaced by *stagnation*. So we are witnessing a situation in which the capitalist syndrome of growth/profits/competition/countervailing power seems to be in process of being replaced by a 'stagflationist' syndrome, made up of cost inflation/subsidy/monopoly/stagnation.

Of course, the last paragraph represents a gross over-simplification of a complex situation, and the 'stagflationist' syndrome is perhaps a caricature of where we are at. Nevertheless, if one examines the market environment in which most enterprises are operating today in the western world, it will be seen to contain as many elements of the second syndrome as of the first. Business finds itself, in other words, poised uneasily between two worlds: the capitalist world of easy certainties to which it hankers to return, and the much more complex, politicised world with which it is having to come to terms.

Capitalism without Profits

The most obvious feature of the changing environment is the decline in profits. In the past, a modest inflation has been held to stimulate profits. On the one hand, it boosts final demand for goods and services. At the same time, it shifts wealth from lenders to borrowers, and thus makes it easier for firms to finance their operations on borrowed money (which they will, of course, repay in depreciated currency).

The post-Keynesian inflation has not had such beneficial characteristics. As we have seen, it has not been a period of buoyant demand in real, as opposed to money, terms. In the later years consumers, faced with a high degree of job insecurity, have preferred to save their money, despite the rapid rate of depreciation, rather than spend it. Moreover, firms have not found it easy to pass on the full amount of cost increases—partly because they under-estimated them in the early stages of the inflation, partly because in some cases they were committed to long-term fixed-price contracts, and partly because governments imposed price controls in attempts to halt the inflationary spiral.

In the UK, as a consequence of all these factors, company profitability in real terms fell from around 10% return on capital in the 1960s to about 2% by the mid-1970s. The development of inflation accounting (which values assets in terms of replacement cost rather than their historical cost) has revealed the extent of the run-down of the capital structure of business, most dramatically in the UK and Italy, but in varying degrees throughout the whole of the industrialised world—leaving aside those businesses which, as we have seen, have dropped out of the private sector altogether.

The decline in the productivity of capital in the western world was not entirely due to the causes described so far in this book. Even in the early 1960s, before the upsurge of inflation, there had been evidence of some decline, as the post-war reconstruction boom began to peter out, and signs of surplus capacity had begun to emerge in a number of key industries (and as newly-industrialising countries outside western Europe and North America began to emerge as increasingly serious competitors). It is quite possible that, even without the pressures recorded in this book, the capitalist world would have entered a period of lower growth in the late 1960s and 1970s, as a reaction to the enormous investment boom of the 1950s and early 1960s. What is clear is that any such tendencies were enormously strengthened and accelerated by the social pressures, and by the attempts of government to contain them at the expense of the business sector.

The result of the abrupt decline in profitability was inevitably a cut-back in investment by industry, which in turn led to higher unemployment. Business faced an intense cash 'squeeze' during the mid-1970s as orders dried up, costs continued to rise, and such funds as were available for investment tended to be syphoned off by government—as we saw in the last chapter—to finance their own soaring spending programmes. The result of the competition of the State for money was to push up interest rates to a point at which enterprises found it virtually impossible to compete effectively for available funds.

The decline in profitability may or may not prove a lasting phenomenon. There are signs that in the late 1970s it could be reversed, as governments everywhere are becoming aware of the fragile nature of their private-sector productive systems. But the role of profits within the economic system, as a measure of performance and a means for moving resources into their most productive uses, may be a more permanent casualty. For what has happened, in the partial replacement of the capitalist by the 'stagflationist' syndrome, is that the rules of the game have been radically changed. The profits which an enterprise makes in present-day circumstances are less likely to reflect its efficiency than the accident of whether or not it is in a sector of the economy which the State is seeking to control. The less 'visible' a business is, the more likely it is to be allowed to make good profits.

Business Objectives in the Mixed Economy
Within the capitalist world, as a consequence of the decline of the Keynesian system, there is great confusion over the objectives which businesses should seek to pursue. For the reasons mentioned above, profitability by itself no longer seems an adequate objective. On the one hand, it is at least as likely today to reflect political as efficiency factors. High recorded profits can be politically

dangerous, for they are likely to attract the attention of governments, who may then seek to impose price controls on the enterprise. Equally, profits have been under attack as contributing to inflation, and as indicating a lack of sensitivity in some cases to external costs like environmental pollution.

But, if a firm is not to seek to maximise its financial return, how is it to measure its performance? How is it to assess the work of its individual profit-responsible managers, and how is it to attract capital from the stock exchanges and banks? It is no accident that it has been during the period of the post-Keynesian inflation that the debate has started in earnest in the west on the *social responsibilities* of business, and on techniques of social audit and social accounting.

The problem can be clearly stated. Business enterprises are part of society. Not only do they produce the bulk of the wealth in society—by generating goods and services and by providing employment—but they also profoundly influence the environment within which they operate, physically and culturally. Society in every western country today has multiple objectives. The single-minded pursuit of economic growth is no longer acceptable. There is growing concern with the *quality of life*, which includes the quality of the environment (the presence or absence of pollution, for example), the quality of the products traded (e.g. the extent to which they meet standards of safety and consumer satisfaction), and the quality of working life (which I will be discussing later in this chapter).

It is reasonable that the business enterprise should include among its objectives the satisfaction of these desires. Indeed, the further the economy moves away from the capitalist and towards the 'stagflationist' syndrome, the more important should social objectives logically become in the business world. One could indeed envisage a situation, in a society where there was no growth, no competition and no distributed profits—so that the business sector financed itself by retained earnings and State subsidy—where enterprises were judged, and judged themselves, entirely by their achievement of agreed social objectives. Such a society would be a long way from any capitalist, or any Marxist, society known to history; but it is by no means inconceivable, nor is there any reason why a business community could not adjust to it (though it would no doubt be irksome and almost certainly inefficient), provided the rules of the game were clearly spelt out and agreed. (Such an economy would of course be highly static and non-innovative.)

However, that is not the situation facing us today, and most likely it is one we shall never encounter in reality. We are likely to continue to subsist in a mixed economy, with a *mélange* of economic and social goals. This means that business has to articulate a set of objectives, for itself as a collectivity and for its individual managers in their respective roles, which will reflect this *mélange*. But this is easier said than done.

Economic objectives—financial targets, market share and sales targets, production targets—have the merit of being both clear and quantifiable. Accountants can measure performance against them without difficulty (albeit sometimes with the aid of a little subterfuge), managers can identify with them and accept to be judged by their success or otherwise in attaining them. But when we move on to social objectives, we are in a much fuzzier world.

First, to what elements in society should the enterprise respond? One school of thought argues that the enterprise should see itself as responsible not just to its investors—which is how company law in the UK and most other western countries requires it to see itself—but to a number of different 'stakeholders', of whom the investor (whether shareholder or fixed-interest lender) is only one. The other major stakeholders are the employees, both managers and workers, whose interest in the company, it can be argued plausibly, is at least as great as those who have lent it money; consumers; suppliers; and the community at large, whether it be the local community or communities in which the enterprise operates, or the larger community represented by the State (or, in the case of multinational companies, many States).

The Enterprise and its 'Stakeholders'

The 'stakeholder' concept, which sees the firm as the centre of a network of conflicting claims and interests, to be balanced one against the other, is a far cry from the traditional doctrine of capitalism, which sees the entrepreneur as an individual using borrowed funds—for which he is legally responsible to the owners—to create wealth. It recognises that the large enterprise is an institution in society, whose activities profoundly affect that society in many ways. It sees the enterprise as a citizen, with the rights and responsibilities of a citizen; entitled to some degree of protection if it falls on hard times, but in return expected to conform to the standards required of a responsible citizen.

It should perhaps be pointed out that this whole approach presupposes a separation between the functions of ownership and control—between those who invest their money in the enterprise and those who manage it. This separation normally exists today in large businesses in western society. In the small business sector, where those who own the business often manage it as well—for example in the family business, farm or shop—the issue of social responsibility in this sense hardly arises.

Even in the large enterprise sector, there are some major difficulties about the stakeholder concept. One can accept that the managers of the enterprise must, if they are to carry out their responsibilities, maintain a balance between the demands of the stakeholders. The investor is entitled to a reasonable return on his money, and to access to information which will enable him to make rational choices about the disposal of his funds. The worker is entitled, not only to reasonable standards of wages and working conditions (I leave the definition of this till later in the chapter), but also to a reasonable say in the operations of the enterprise as they directly affect him or her. The consumer is entitled to products which give value for money, do not contain health or safety risks, and which are honestly and accurately described in advertising and sales material. He or she is entitled to expect full and speedy redress for product or service failures; and that the company does not deliberately build obsolescence into its product.

The supplier is entitled to fair treatment and to avoidance of exploitation by a monopoly buyer, and to be kept informed wherever possible on aspects of the company's future plans which could affect him. The local community is entitled to guarantees that the enterprise will not damage the environment in which it works, but rather that it will contribute, as a good citizen should, to the improvement of the community; and at national level (and international level where multinationals are concerned) governments are entitled to the same assurances, and to see that enterprises meet all proper legal and social obligations.[1]

One can accept that it is for the directors of the enterprise to assess these various and in some cases mutually conflicting obligations, and to try to strike the best balance in each case. In my own view it is easier to do this in a two-tier board structure, such as exists in West Germany and certain other Continental countries, than in unitary board structures as in the Anglo-Saxon and French company law systems. A two-tier board enables one to separate the supervisory functions which we have just been describing from the executive function of actually running the business. However, separation of the supervisory and executive functions does not absolutely require the formal establishment of two parallel board structures. There are many ways in which the separate functions can be exercised within a unitary board system; what is important is not to separate institutions, but clearly to distinguish and separate the functions.

But the question then arises of whether, and if so how and how many of, the stakeholders should be formally represented in the supervisory structure. So far the debate has tended to focus on representation of one stakeholder only—the employee. The case for trade union representation on industry boards has been argued at length of late throughout western Europe. Such representation formally exists in West Germany, the Netherlands, Austria, Denmark, Sweden, Norway and Luxembourg, and is under active discussion in the UK, France, Belgium and Ireland. The main arguments concern, not the principle, but rather the role of the worker-director. Is he to be elected by the workers, or appointed

by trade union machinery? Can non-unionised employees partici-
pate in his selection? Is he to have the same responsibilities, once
chosen, as other directors, or is he to see himself primarily as a
representative of the workers (in which case the boardroom becomes an extension of the collective bargaining system)? Is the
appointment of worker-directors to be mandatory, or only if the
workers ask for it? The answers to these questions, which in my
view are crucial in determining the success or failure of this great
experiment in industrial democracy, have to be considered in the
overall context of the demands of the labour movement for
changes in industrial structure, which will occupy us in the second
half of this chapter.

But, assuming agreement can be reached on worker participation in the boardroom, what of the other stakeholders? In most
companies the investor is already represented, explicitly or im-
plicitly, by one or more directors. No great difficulty of principle
arises in considering formal representation of the public interest,
whether local or national, though there might be all kinds of
practical objections (not least that of whether the 'public interest'
director should assume the same obligations as his colleagues for
the viability of the enterprise, or whether he should limit himself
to seeing that the enterprise conformed to national or local policy
objectives). The question becomes more difficult when one moves
to the other stakeholders—consumers and suppliers. Indeed, one
can wonder whether these should have formal right of representation at all, since their relationship with the enterprise is a limited
contractual one, and their redress for grievances normally lies
through the market (in other words they can stop buying and
selling, and switch their custom to others).[2]

In short, there is a built-in asymmetry in the stakeholder concept. Some stakeholders are more equal than others, and some
can less easily be accommodated through a representational structure than others. (One can of course envisage special panels or
consultative committees to consider and adjudicate on supplier
and customer claims.) More fundamental are the problems of the
accountability of directors drawn from the stakeholders. They

must represent their clients' interests, but they must also accept a general responsibility for the survival and prosperity of the enterprise, which may from time to time conflict with the representational role. And with multinational companies there are special problems. If the public interest, and/or trade union interests, in one country are represented on the board of directors of the parent company, how can this right be denied to representatives of the same interest in other countries of operation? But if the right is extended to a number of countries, the board becomes an unmanageable battlefield of conflicting interests and claims.

In addition to problems over stakeholder representation, there are a range of questions concerning the measurement of social objectives. Financial, marketing and production objectives are readily quantifiable. So they can be easily incorporated into budgets and corporate plans, against the achievement of which management's performance can be monitored and judged. In the social field it is vastly more difficult. One can measure, negatively, certain kinds of social objectives. Industrial disputes, labour turnover and absenteeism are all indications of worker alienation which suggest a low rate of internal social performance. Accidents at work, numbers of workers being trained, employment of members of minority groups, are all indicators—however rough and ready—which can be fed into a social accounting matrix. As regards external social responsibility, the standard of pollution control is clearly relevant, though more for some companies than others.

However, all these—and other elements which could be thrown in—fail to add up to a quantifiable system of objectives to match the traditional trio of finance, marketing and production. It is hard, given the present state of accounting expertise, to build into the management reporting system a set of social objectives which will adequately reflect the evolving role of the business enterprise in post-Keynesian society. For some time to come, therefore, it is probable that management performance in western society will suffer from a certain confusion of objectives, and a lack of clarity and understanding as to what values the business sector should be seeking to optimise.

The Claims of Industrial Democracy

Business, therefore, suffers at the present time from uncertainties about its social function, as well as from serious constraints on finance. At the same time it is at the receiving end of a mounting crescendo of demands from its work-force for radical changes in the organisation and command structure of industry. These demands have been presented in parallel with, though separately from, the pressures for higher wages which have already been noted. They derive in large measure from the same sources: an increasing unwillingness to accept the type of working conditions and environment previously thought necessary to the successful production of goods and services in capitalist industrial society, and the higher standards of education and expectations among the work-force.

This has led to non-wage demands which can be classified as follows: demands for *job security, industrial democracy* and *work humanisation*. It will be useful to discuss each of these in turn, recognising however that there is considerable overlap between them.

The demand that the worker, in return for loyalty to the firm, should enjoy security of employment—a degree of security increasing with age and length of service—is not new to western democracy. It is one of the pillars of the Japanese socio-industrial system, and the evidence suggests that in Japan it has contributed to worker satisfaction and identification with the enterprise, and thus to labour flexibility within the firm. On the other hand, it has meant that when recession strikes the Japanese economy, employers are unable to react by cutting their labour force, and are driven therefore to cover their overheads by expanding foreign sales, which they can subsidise from a protected home market. The western democracies, with their more open domestic markets, are not able to react to trade fluctuations in the Japanese style. But in western Europe and North America, too, union and governmental pressures have been forcing firms to accept higher and higher penalties for dismissing workers, buttressed in some countries by elaborate appeals procedures which can delay, and in some cases countermand, the redundancy. The net effect, as we have seen, has been to convert labour increasingly from a variable to a fixed cost, and to make employers more reluctant to take on new workers. In the west, as in Japan, there are emerging signs of a 'split' labour market, divided between those workers who are employed in large enterprises which can offer a high degree of job security, and those in less sheltered employment or un-employed.

Not surprisingly, the pressure for job security has grown as unemployment has increased. It is likely, however, to remain a permanent feature in the post-Keynesian economy—though, un-like in Japan, it will probably be accompanied by continuing labour mobility in western Europe and North America. In other words, in these societies it is likely to be seen as an unconditional right of labour, rather than a reciprocal feudal-type obligation as between master and servant.

It is significant that the demand for greater industrial democ-racy, so strident in the western democracies, has as yet evoked few echoes in Japan. And indeed, within the western democracies, there have been very significant differences in the nature of the demands made. The pressure for worker participation in decision-making at boardroom level, for example, hardly exists at all in North America, or anywhere else outside western Europe. Even in western Europe, it is little felt in the Latin countries—except, very recently, in France. Trade unions with a Marxist tradition, such as those which dominate in France and Italy, tend to regard participation in the boardrooms of capitalist enterprises as a class betrayal—and it is naturally in these countries that employer opposition to such participation is also strongest.

It is in those countries where social consensus is highest—West Germany, the Netherlands, Scandinavia—that the trade unions have tended to set the highest value on securing representation at board level, and it is in these countries that the resistance of em-ployers has been weakest. We shall return to this question in Chapter 8, when we will consider the role of worker participation in helping to build a policy of social consensus. But we should notice here the attitudes of two other major groups of unions, which differ both from the 'participative' Nordics and the Marxist Latins. The prevailing attitude among the British, Irish and Belgian trade unions is that participation at board level should be sought, but not at the price of any change in collective bargaining objectives. Rather, membership of boards should be used as a bargaining weapon to strengthen the position of workers *vis-à-vis* management. This is directly contrary to the prevailing practice in those Continental countries where boardroom participation is well established, where the unions accept that participation in decision-making involves responsibilities as well as rights, and where in some cases worker-elected directors have been accused by their former colleagues of ignoring their interests and 'selling out'.

A significant minority of British unions—and virtually all unions in North America and Australasia—argue that there is a fundamental incompatibility between the management and the trade union function, and that unions should therefore concentrate on securing their demands through collective bargaining, and not be seduced into participation in managerial decision-making.

Opinion in trade unions is very fluid as regards the whole question of boardroom participation—or power-sharing, as it might more properly be called. But the argument is essentially over means, not ends. In all countries trade unions over the last decade have been mounting a sustained attack on the prerogatives of management, seeking to make the command structure in business less autocratic, to replace management by edict with management by consent. Whether the means chosen are institutionalised power-sharing, government legislation, collective bargaining pressures, or a combination of these, the objective is the same.

Thus in all western countries there has grown up over the post-war period a more and more comprehensive body of labour law, which seeks to protect the rights of employees against the exercise of arbitrary management power. In Sweden legislation approved in 1976 specifically delineates those areas in which management is free to take decisions unilaterally, and those where it can only move after agreement with the unions. In Sweden, Denmark, the Netherlands and West Germany measures have been prepared which would oblige firms to divert a certain proportion of their profits every year into trade union-managed investment funds which would then be reinvested in industry; so that eventually the trade unions would become the biggest shareholders in the private sector. (They already exercise considerable influence in all western countries, not least the USA, through the investments of their pension funds.)

Thus, in the post-Keynesian world, power over the private sector of business—at least as far as the large firms are concerned—is increasingly having to be shared between capital and labour, and as labour itself becomes a major owner of capital the traditional social dividing lines are becoming blurred. At the same time, management is having to become much more democratic and participative in style, and many of the traditional class structures within industry—the division between white-collar and blue-collar workers, for example—are disappearing. The process is not a painless one, and for one grade—the junior managers, foremen or supervisors—it is proving traumatic. These grades have lost much of their former authority, they tend to find themselves squeezed between the big power-blocs of top management and the shop stewards, their differentials in countries operating wages policies are being eroded, and many of their older members are less educated than the workers they are trying to control. Their position in the post-Keynesian world of the mid-1970s is far from enviable.

Alienation on the Shopfloor

There is of course no necessary connection between industrial democracy on the shopfloor and trade union representation in the boardroom. There are many examples of firms with highly participative structures at shopfloor level and traditional-style boards, and others whose boardrooms are graced with union officials but who nevertheless operate rigid, hierarchical and authoritarian command structures down the line. From the point of view of the shopfloor worker, more important than power-sharing at board level is the existence of an effective system of works councils or *comités d'entreprise* which can influence decision-making at the level of the individual worker, and act as a two-way channel of communication.

It is at this level that the key issues which determine the quality of working life—remuneration and fringe benefits, job structuring, health, safety, amenities, training and promotion, hours of work and holidays, grievance procedures and the like—can best be dealt with. These issues, particularly those concerned with work structuring, are becoming increasingly important, as a richer, better-educated, more demanding society is increasingly questioning the concept of 'work' as a necessary evil. Hence the growing importance of investments designed to humanise work itself, through autonomous work groups, job enrichment or job enlargement schemes, and the like.[3]

This process has so far made its biggest impact in Scandinavia, though experiments in work humanisation are also taking place on a substantial scale in West Germany and the USA, and on a smaller scale in many other countries, including the UK, the Netherlands, Australia, France and Italy. In Norway successful experiments have been carried out over a number of years in various industries, under the joint supervision of employers and unions. In Sweden employers have taken the initiative, with union support, in promoting work humanisation in a number of key industries, often involving major capital investments. The most dramatic investment to date has been the new car plant of Volvo at Kalmar, a plant which moves right away from the assembly-line concept and instead relies on autonomous work groups, with a high degree of flexibility as to their method of work, to assemble the cars. In some respects—notably the planning of the work by computer—the technology employed is very advanced. But in other respects it represents an apparent step backwards, in which the productivity both of the worker and of the capital installed seems to be somewhat below that of best standards in traditional assembly-line work.[4]

On the other hand, Kalmar scores heavily on job satisfaction, as is shown by improvements in quality and reduced turnover and absenteeism compared to Volvo's more orthodox plants (in Sweden, but not abroad). The reason for the Kalmar investment was simply that, with the development of higher education in Sweden, it was becoming more and more difficult to get Swedes to accept the monotony of work on the assembly line, no matter how high the wage. The result was high and mounting absenteeism and labour turnover, and a fall in product quality. It is too soon to say whether Kalmar is the right answer, but there is no doubt about the existence of the problem.

Nor is it limited to Sweden. In the UK the car industry is notoriously prone to strikes of a peculiarly stupid and vicious kind. In the US the brand-new assembly-line plant of General Motors at Lordstown was subject during the early 1970s to a process of strikes, absenteeism and industrial sabotage only explicable in terms of an almost pathological alienation on the part of many workers.

It is true that one does not get the same complaints from the car plants of West Germany, France, Italy or Belgium. The reason is that these plants are staffed to a very high degree by migrant workers (in Fiat's case, from Sicily, Sardinia and Calabria), whose expectations and cultural standards are much lower. But, as migrants cease to play such a big part in Europe's economy (and as their own standards rise), the problems of shopfloor alienation which perturb the Scandinavians are going to bulk larger and larger in the thinking of their southern and western neighbours too. The likelihood is that in the 1980s a significant part of the new investment being undertaken in European and American industry will be designed, not to raise productivity or expand capacity, but to humanise the factory environment in the least attractive industries in order to counter worker alienation. Such investments could take the form of automating the unattractive jobs, or of trying to make them more interesting, as the Scandinavians have sought to do.

Industry, in short, is undergoing a ferment of change. Both internally and externally, it has to satisfy demands which even a few years ago had barely been articulated. In Europe the main pressure for change is coming from the unions and the shopfloor. In North America it is the external pressure groups—the consumers, the conservationists—who are making more of the running. The biggest immediate challenge facing European managers is the demand for power-sharing from the unions. For American managers the bigger threat is the spread of legislation, curbing and restricting the power of business to operate with its traditional freedom.

One of the main reasons for this difference in the social climate on the two sides of the Atlantic is the more limited conception of their role in society taken by the US unions. Compared to their European counterparts, they are less ideological, more pragmatic, more businesslike in their approach and objectives. They do not see themselves, nor are they seen by their fellow-citizens, as natural vehicles for social advance. They are perceived rather as powerful but limited pressure groups, and as beneficiaries of the industrial system. They would not therefore normally be expected to champion the cause of the consumer or other groups, whose interest might be seen as contrary to that of an expanding, profitable—and therefore high-wage-paying—business sector. In a word, the typical US trade union is oriented towards welfare capitalism, not towards Marxism or any other brand of socialism. So the radicals who seek to reform the business system, who in the European environment find natural allies in the trade union movement, in North America have to draw their support from other elements, such as the consumerist and environmentalist movements.

This is a very important social difference today. But for how long will it last? If European legislation compels multi-national companies operating on both sides of the Atlantic to put European trade union representatives on their boards of directors, is it conceivable that US unions will be content to remain indefinitely in a disenfranchised, and therefore disadvantaged, situation? For there is little doubt that the composition of the board of directors in a multinational can significantly affect the pattern of its investment. Worker representatives from country A will do their best to see that their countrymen get a good share of the capital investment and job opportunities in the firm's expansion plans; if country B is not represented at the highest decision-making levels, the key investment decisions are likely to go against it, in default of overwhelmingly convincing economic arguments. It is this politicising of decision-making, arising from the growth of worker participation in Europe, which more than any other factor is likely to weaken the flexibility, and therefore the effectiveness, of multinational enterprises over the next decade.

Experience in the post-war world suggests that ideas travel with remarkable speed, and that there is a process of upward convergence in the demands that different societies make on their productive sectors. So it would be rash to assume that Europe will long remain immune from the virus of militant consumerism, or America from that of union demands for power-sharing. In all post-Keynesian societies the business sector is on the defensive. The demands with which it is faced will not disappear—nor should they, for in almost every case they are legitimate expressions of the aspirations of a society reaching out for a better quality of life-style. What *is* urgent is that there should be some ordering of the priorities, that businessmen should be told clearly and coherently what society expects of them, and that they should then be given the means whereby these expectations can be fulfilled. Otherwise the frustrations of society will continue to mount, and the baleful implications—as we shall see in the next chapter—may invade and infect ever wider areas of an already demoralised and damaged civilisation.

NOTES TO CHAPTER 4

[1] The extent to which society now expects business enterprises to assume social responsibilities is indicated by a series of public opinion polls undertaken in the U S by the Harris Poll organisation in 1966, 1971 and 1972. The poll asked respondents in what areas they thought businessmen and companies should 'give some special leadership'. In 1966 69% of the respondents thought business should give a lead in controlling air and water pollution; 76% in

eliminating economic depressions; 74% in 'rebuilding our cities'; 73% in enabling people to use their creative talents fully; 69% in eliminating racial discrimination and 'wiping out poverty.'; 43% in raising living standards around the world; 63% in finding cures for disease; 71% in giving a college education to all qualified; 42% in controlling crime; 50% in cutting down highway accidents; 48% in raising moral standards; 55% in reducing the threat of war; and 37% in eliminating religious prejudice. In the 1972 poll the answers to the same questions were, respectively, 92%, 88%, 85%, 85%, 84%, 83%, 80%, 76%, 75%, 73%, 72%, 70%, 68% and 63%. On every single issue the proportions expecting a lead from business had risen sharply in the six years. (In 1966 only 17% of the respondents thought business should give a lead in 'controlling too rapid population growth'; by 1972 44% thought it should.)

2 Of course, in the 'stagflationist' syndrome, or in any other situation where there is a high degree of monopoly control of the market, the consumer loses his sovereignty and cannot effectively seek redress for his grievances through the market.

3 Such investments have a social as well as an economic importance. The effects of alienation and boredom on the shopfloor or in the office spread outside the business environment. Sometimes a bored, demotivated worker can find compensation for his or her frustrations outside work—in the family, in leisure or social activities. But by no means always. A bored, frustrated worker can too easily become an apathetic, anti-social, sometimes a violent, citizen.

4 There is a good deal of dubiety in these comparisons. A joint employer-union investigative team has estimated that 'efficiency at Kalmar is equal to or better than Volvo's conventional assembly facilities in Sweden', but that 'the investment cost for the Kalmar plant was 10% above that for a conventional plant'. The report finds that the overall standard of worker satisfaction was much higher at Kalmar than elsewhere. (*The Volvo Kalmar Plant*—a report by the Rationalisation Council.)

5
Symptoms of
Social Breakdown

In the four preceding chapters I have diagnosed the sickness of contemporary society as being the disparity between the claims being made on the productive system and its ability, at current levels of technology, to meet them. I have sought to explain *why* there should have been this sudden convergence of demands at this precise moment of history; and I have traced the effect of the most important set of demands—those associated with monetary rewards and the status of workers—on the State and the industrial system.

It will no doubt be argued by some that what I have been describing is not a crisis of industrial society as such, but specifically a crisis of *capitalism*[1]—a crisis from which the Marxist economies of the Communist world are immune. It is necessary to examine this claim before we proceed any further, for if it is true, the implications are of course rather important. Can it be that we are now witnessing the final collapse of capitalism under the weight of its internal contradictions, so often foretold by Marxist thinkers?

There is indeed some *prima facie* evidence to support such a thesis. Certainly the nations of the Soviet bloc (I explicitly exclude Yugoslavia from this group, for reasons which will appear shortly) have not experienced the fantastic inflation rates suffered by capitalist economies. That is because they do not have free trade unions with the right to strike, and because they control both wages and prices. So one might argue that the disease (if it can be so called) is a fever of democracy, rather than of capitalism. For there is little evidence that the peoples of the Soviet bloc are any less materialistic than their brothers and sisters in the western democracies, or that the gap between ambitions and achievement is any less on the Soviet side of the Iron Curtain.

As regards materialism, it was indeed Karl Marx who first described religion as 'the opium of the people', and Marxism is the child of Victorian scientific determinism, claiming to substitute a genuine earthly paradise, through social engineering, for a spurious heavenly one. It has demonstrably failed to do so to the satisfaction of most of its people, otherwise it would hardly be necessary to buttress the political regime by an onerous apparatus of police surveillance, the continued denial of civil liberties, control over incomes and most other aspects of the economic system, and strict limitation on foreign travel.

Despite these restrictions, the Soviet bloc has not been able to avoid entirely the contagion of rising expectations. Worker alienation has assumed substantial proportions in the USSR and its East European satellites. Revolts against the system have taken place in East Germany in 1953, in Hungary in 1956, in Czechoslovakia in 1968; in each case they were forcibly suppressed. In Poland unofficial strikes brought down the unpopular Gomulka regime when it tried to remove food subsidies in 1970, and prevented the succeeding Gierek government from carrying through similar measures in 1976. The result is that Poland's economy remains in heavy deficit on its foreign trade.

Recent studies—notably *The Roots of Inflation*, a collection of essays by eight international economists, published by Wilton House in 1975—suggest that the inflation problem in the Soviet bloc countries is much more like that in the west than is commonly realised. The characteristic of these economies is endemic suppressed inflation, resulting in persistent hoarding, shortages of final goods, queues and black markets, with periodic substantial price increases to correct the worst distortions which have been allowed to build up in the system. These problems have become more acute as living standards have risen and consumers have become more discriminating in their tastes—so that shortages of badly-wanted goods go hand-in-hand with the surplus production of goods which can no longer be sold to a more demanding public. As in the west, managers and governments have sought to buy their way out of trouble by allowing wages to rise faster than productivity—managers in order that they can attract or retain scarce labour, and thus fulfil their production norms within the State planning system, governments in order to head off possible unrest (which cannot be entirely discounted even in police states). As in the west, the rise in wages resulting from 'cost-push' leads to increased purchasing power, and hence to reinforcing 'demand-pull' inflation. So the inflationary spiral operates in planned as well as in market economies. And the more the planned economies try to introduce more market-orientation into their systems, giving their managers more freedom to respond to market forces and more profit-responsibility, the greater the danger of the suppressed inflation becoming open (as indeed has happened in Yugoslavia). The greater the distortions which have been allowed to accumulate as a result of economic controls, the harder it is to remove the controls without an explosion.

All the available evidence suggests, therefore, that the pressures which have shaken western capitalism are at work, albeit suppressed, within the Soviet bloc.[2] The fact that they have been slower to manifest themselves is partly due to the repressive forces of the police state, and the absence of a free trade union movement; partly to the fact that the mass media in these countries act as transmitters of State ideology, and not, as in the west, as stimuli of consumer wants; and partly because there is, paradoxically, less movement between the classes, less social mobility, less opportunity for personal advancement, than in the western democracies.

All the striving, the tension that one finds west of the Iron Curtain is replaced in the Soviet world by a surly acquiescence in the established order. But the traveller does not have to look far to encounter the tensions beneath the surface. What does not seem to exist, at least in European Communism, is any counter-ideology, any sense of social purpose to set off against the admitted frustration of individual aspirations. Maybe the absence of any genuine collectivist spirit reflects, not just the ideological barrenness of Marxist social engineering, but the individualistic spirit of

Christian civilisation. For in the civilisations of the Far East—Chinese and Japanese—one does indeed find it. One finds it not only in Communist China, but also in different forms in capitalist Japan, and in the overseas Chinese communities which are also highly capitalistic in spirit. In these and the neighbouring communities, such as South Korea, one encounters a high degree of communal solidarity and a work ethic which resembles that of nineteenth-century England. It is these countries, under whatever regime they live, which seem best to have avoided the symptoms of social breakdown which afflict the once Christian west. So the crisis which we have been describing in earlier chapters can perhaps better be explained as the decay of the Christian individualist tradition than as a disease of capitalism. Those cultures and societies which have traditionally put a higher value on social cohesion and conformity than on individual liberty have tended, at least up to now, to cope much better with the stresses of the post-Keynesian era. The implications of this for us in the west will be discussed in Chapters 8 and 9.

Yet it is not entirely true that these stresses are a disease of democracy. It is true that democracies are less able to contain the stresses, because they lack the instruments of repression. They do not have the means, unlike the dictatorships of Eastern Europe, Latin America, or (as far as the black majority is concerned) South Africa, to torture or shoot trade union leaders. That is of course a serious limitation when one is facing problems of wage inflation. Yet the history of the last ten years shows that democratic political structures do have a remarkable resilience. Inflations of 20% a year or more may make them bend, but they do not break them. No single democracy in the industrialised world has yet succumbed to dictatorship, whether of Left or Right, in the last decade. That is something which few people would have been prepared to bet on ten years ago, had they foreseen the strains which these democracies were about to undergo. What is more, three countries—Greece, Portugal and Spain—in the same period have moved out of the shadow of totalitarianism into the democratic camp.

One may also remark on the surprising ability of the European Economic Community, during this traumatic period, not only to maintain intact the free trade systems of the common market, without a retreat into national autarky or sectional protectionism, but actually to expand from six member-states to nine. In other words, the post-Keynesian stresses have not yet undermined the structure of the democratic nation-state, nor shattered the liberal world trading system created in the Keynesian heyday after 1945.

Centrifugal Forces

But one cannot be complacent. For it is evident today that the forces of liberalism, internationalism and democracy are on the defensive. Progress on the further stages of European integration in the EEC structure has virtually halted since the enlargement of the Community in 1972. Respect for the authority of the State is everywhere diminished. Separatist forces, often violent in nature, have sprung up among minority groups in many countries. In Northern Ireland, Quebec, Scotland, Corsica, Catalonia and the Basque country, once quiescent minorities are asserting their rights against the nation-state. One of the great problems confronting all modern governments is the extent to which, and the methods by which, authority can be devolved to local and regional communities.

A country which has adopted one of the most radical solutions to this problem is, ironically, the maverick of the Communist world, Yugoslavia. Not only does Yugoslavia have a federal system of government, with considerable powers devolved to the regional administrations, it has also introduced a system of worker control in its major industrial enterprises. In Yugoslavia the capitalist owner-boss has been replaced, not—as in the Soviet bloc—by a technocrat responsible to the State, but by a manager responsible to a workers' elected committee. Industrial democracy, in short, has been carried to its logical conclusion (though enterprises still draw a substantial part of their capital from the State's financial institutions, and they have to conform to a rather rudimentary State planning system).

The results have not been an unmixed success. Yugoslavia has suffered as severely as any western democracy from wage inflation, and from the other western evil of unbalanced regional development—though it has also enjoyed a rather rapid growth rate (but not more than the strictly-controlled Marxist economies of Romania and Bulgaria).

The demands for greater regional and local autonomy now being encountered in a growing number of countries reflect, in part, disenchantment with the performance of the nation-state in countering the post-Keynesian stresses reviewed in Chapter 3. Remote bureaucratic systems can be tolerated, grudgingly, if they appear to be operating efficiently and fairly. If they are inefficient and apparently unjust, their remoteness becomes an added insult. By definition, if they are failing to deal justly with *me* and mine, they must be giving too much to *you* and yours. So I need a system of government which will be closer to me, and which I can therefore keep under closer scrutiny.

In earlier chapters I analysed the collapse of the Keynesian system in terms of *hubris* and *nemesis*. Governments came to believe that they could control the economic system in such a way as to meet all claims made upon it. As a result, the claims escalated to a point at which the system could no longer deliver the goods. Governments therefore became discredited, in a way which their nineteenth-century forebears—who did not believe, and did not claim, that they could control economic forces—would have avoided.

Exactly the same explanation can be applied to the broader field of social policy. In the post-war era governments have come to believe that they can solve the social (and to a large extent the *personal*) problems of their citizens, by techniques of social engineering and the application of ever greater doses of social support. In many cases governments have thought that they were applying once-for-all aid to solve a specific social problem, only to discover that this solution produced a new set of problems, so that the commitment became an unending one. Thus, when the British National Health Service was set up, it was assumed that after an initial heavy burst of spending to raise the nation's standards of health, there would be a reduction in commitments because healthy people would not need medicine. In fact, spending on public health—not just in the UK but in all western countries—has been one of the fastest-rising sectors of expenditure year after year. The appetite for medical care grows with eating.

Again, the solution of one social problem tends to breed another. Slums have been cleared to make way for new, hygienic, high-rise apartments. This has created new problems of neurosis, alienation and the breakdown of community life. New job opportunities have been found for women. This has produced a growing problem of juvenile delinquency among their children, no longer under continuous parental care and surveillance. No section of the Welfare State has grown faster than the provision of personal social services; their clients are the old, problem families and their children, house-bound invalids, and the like. Clearly these social workers are filling a vacuum, and clearly the demand for their services is still greater than the supply. But what happened before the personal social services were created? Who performed the tasks they are now doing?

The answer is that their work was done, with varying degrees of adequacy, by families, by the Church, by local communities. The State is trying to fill the vacuum created by the decline or transformation of these institutions in modern society. That it does so inadequately, despite the enormous and growing expenditure devoted to it, is evidenced by the increasing incidence of violence and delinquency in western society as a whole. The situation is at its worst in the decaying urban centres, where environmental blight and the decline of community life are negating the work of the State welfare services, whose activities in any case often seem ill-planned and mutually conflicting.

Families and Communities

The State, in other words, does not cut a very convincing figure as Santa Claus. Plainly many of the tasks performed, at great cost, by well-meaning officials could be much better done by self-reliant local communities, and by extended families. As regards the family, the issue, as we have seen already, is an immensely complex one. It would be totally retrograde to deny women the liberation which has been achieved, though as yet imperfectly, as regards their right to work and to earn an income independent of their husband or mate. But it is foolish to shut our eyes to the social cost which this liberation can bring in its wake, in terms of the decline of the family as a self-sufficient unit, and the alienation of the 'latchkey' child, who can easily become tomorrow's delinquent. The solution must lie in giving the woman a freer choice. If she wishes to work rather than to stay at home and bring up her children, she should be entirely free to do so without any moral hang-ups or guilt feelings. In so far as they can, the authorities—firm or local authority—should provide crèches and other amenities for the child whose parent is working. But she should not be forced or induced into this situation against her will by financial pressure. If she prefers to care for her children, and save the community the expense of so doing, she should be assisted—for example, by some form of home care allowance (failing, of course, a comprehensive 'negative income tax' system, which would be another way of solving the problem); and, once again, she should feel free to take up this option without any moral hang-ups or guilt feelings. The State and society, in other words, should adopt a neutral posture as between the working wife and the housewife. Easy to say, but apparently hard to achieve.

One of the most important changes which has taken place in western society this century has been the displacement of the extended family, embracing several generations, by the nuclear family (parents and children only). The nuclear family itself, as we have seen, is now under strain as a result of women's career aspirations and the changes in morals resulting from medical technology. In Russia, where working wives have been the norm throughout the Soviet era, housework and child-minding has frequently been undertaken by the grandmother, the *babushka*; the extended family of peasant days has adapted itself to an industrial environment. But this has been rare in western Europe or North America. Our societies have tended to use part of the dividend from higher living standards to separate the older generation from their children and grandchildren. As the old are living longer, the social cost of maintaining them has grown steeply—maintaining them not only in material terms, but (and this has proved much more difficult) giving them a *raison d'être* once their traditional family responsibilities have gone. It is our treatment of the old which most shocks students of our culture nurtured outside the western environment.

So there are two deep rifts in our culture today as regards the family. The first is the need to reconcile the aspirations of working women with their responsibilities as wives and mothers. The second is the treatment of the old, whose children are all too ready to transfer their responsibilities for them to a State which is manifestly ill-equipped to carry out such a role. Of the two, the second could prove the more intractable problem.

So far as the community is concerned—whether one is talking of a local community, a region with its own cultural identity, a national group with a distinct heritage and homogeneity—the issues involved are different. On the one hand, certain services have to be provided and organised centrally, if one is to avoid inequalities and achieve the economies of large-scale operation. On the other hand, wherever possible government should be brought closer to the governed, since 'it is only the wearer who knows where the shoe pinches'. Local government in all western democracies is caught between two pressures. On the one hand it is the local arm of the national bureaucracy, dispensing services which are determined at national level. At the same time, it is—or should be—the forum in which local issues, priorities and preoccupations are debated and decided, and where appropriate, transmitted to the national centre.

The problem is, first, to establish clearly what is the appropriate level for decision-making in each subject area. Should housing policy be decided nationally, or locally? Who should settle educational policy, or roads, or the organisation of law and order? The allocation of responsibility between central and local authority over a large area of governmental spending is unclear, not just in the UK but in most western countries. The result is not only an undue amount of confusion and friction between the central and local bureaucracies, but also a considerable degree of duplication of functions, leading to excessive bureaucratic overheads. Western society is becoming endemically 'over-governed'. We need, therefore, a clearer separation of powers between national centre and local authorities; (the issue is of course complicated by the interposition in many cases of regional authorities between national and local levels). The principle to be followed should be that powers should be delegated in all cases *except* (a) where the scale of operation is such that no local authority could command the professional or technical resources to carry it through; (b) where a national interest is clearly involved, as in defence or security, for example; (c) where equity requires a nationally uniform policy, as in the collection of national taxes, or the administration of justice.

We need, also, a clearer separation of functions at local or regional level between the *bureaucratic* role of administering nationally-determined services to the local populace—acting as the local or regional arm of the national bureaucracy; and the *representational* role of dealing with, and responding to, local or regional problems. It is in this second role that one would hope to see a regeneration of local democracy, to fill the vacuum left by the obvious failures of national social engineering—a renaissance of community politics. There is every sign that this is indeed happening.

But we have to be sure that the new vitality of local politics, the growing strength of the various movements for local or regional devolution, contribute to the cohesion of society and not to its decay. On the face of it these movements appear to represent a revitalisation of democracy, a realistic attempt to solve problems which do not lend themselves to 'universalist' national solutions, a means of adjusting national framework policies to meet specific local situations, giving an added dimension of strength and solidity to the nation-state.

That is how it should be; but it is not the way it usually seems to happen. Too often in the last decade devolution movements have resulted in the duplication of the national bureaucracy by local bureaucracies which have all the faults, and few of the virtues, of Big Brother at the centre. This is because the centre has wanted to concede the appearance of power, while retaining the substance. Thus there has been no genuine transference of authority to local level.

Why should this be? The answer, I believe, is that the movement for devolution is normally seen by the central authorities, not as a positive development, but as a threat; and not unreasonably so. For devolution pressures have gathered force at precisely the time when the authority of the State has been challenged by inflation, by the open aggression of pressure groups, and when as we have seen the whole system of public spending has begun to slide out of control. In these circumstances centrifugal forces grow strong, and the reaction of the State—both among politicians and bureaucrats—is to try to cling to the central apparatus of control, for fear of a total break-up of the system.

The conclusion must be that only when health is restored at the centre can the real issues of devolution—the separation of powers in a meaningful and rational way—be discussed and settled objectively. In any other circumstances the whole question becomes a power struggle in which regions and localities strive to escape the control of the centre, and the centre clings to what powers it can retain out of a sense of weakness and fear. That unfortunately is the situation that obtains today. Thus devolutionary pressures are seen as part of the problem of the modern state, when they should more properly be seen as part of the solution. We have to heal the whole before we can safely operate on the parts.

The Crisis of the Nation-State

The trouble is that the nation-state is facing an erosion of sovereignty on three fronts. It is no longer able fully to control the activities of some of its over-mighty subjects—for example the more powerful trade unions (and, one might add, multinational companies operating on its territory). Its failures in this area, as we have seen, have damaged its self-confidence and its credibility. It is facing growing pressures to devolve authority on sub-sections within its territory—whether regional or local. But, thirdly, national autonomy is visibly diminishing in an ever more interdependent, interconnected world. When a country gets into debt, like the UK or Italy, its economic policy, whether it likes it or not, comes under the influence of its creditors. Within the European Community, power is increasingly and irreversibly (if very slowly) moving from national to European level. Already in one major sector, agriculture, the vital decisions on prices and support systems are no longer taken at national level, but at the level of the EEC as a whole. In the not-too-distant future, one can see the British House of Commons having to share power and authority with a directly elected European Parliament on the one hand, and with regional assemblies in Scotland and Wales on the other (and, as we shall see in Chapter 8, also with the great producer interests of the 'Corporate State').

The nation-state as an institution, therefore, appears to be on the decline—and it is important to try to assess, clearly and unemotionally, the reasons why this should be so. Essentially, the nation-state owes its strength as the basic unit of the modern world, to two things: first, in most but not all cases, because it could act as a cultural and political focus for people of common racial stock and/or language, a unit to which they could attach their loyalties and sense of belonging; second, because it represented a unit of the right size and structure to cope with the problems of a rapidly changing world environment, large enough to stand on its own feet and reap the benefits of changing markets and technology, not so large as to be unwieldy and unmanageable.

The upsurge of nationalism during the nineteenth century destroyed some nation-states (e.g. the polyglot Hapsburg empire of Austria-Hungary) and created many others (among them Germany and Italy). In the twentieth century, nationalism has destroyed most of the great colonial empires established between the sixteenth and nineteenth centuries (with the single significant exception of the Soviet Russian empire inherited from the Tsars), and has sown seeds of dissension among the submerged national communities existing within large, comparatively homogeneous nation-states. At the same time the ability of the national bureaucracies to manage change has become increasingly questionable. Many of the problems require a frame of response either much greater or much smaller than that presented by the average nation-state. Thus we need a more flexible decision-making system, in which issues can be dealt with at the appropriate level—local, regional, national, international—for each problem, instead of each decision having to be filtered through the single level of the national bureaucracy.[3]

Unfortunately, words like 'national' and 'bureaucracy' have acquired such a load of emotive overtones that the rational issues involved in discussion about them are easily overlooked. Thus it is perhaps necessary to state that a transfer of responsibility for decision-making in certain cases to lower levels than the national, in others to higher levels, is not an attack on national sovereignty, but an attempt to make the whole system work more effectively. Nothing could be more lethal to national sovereignty than a breakdown of the system due to administrative overload: this is the danger that now threatens.

To say this is not to take an 'anti-bureaucratic' stance. If we want to understand the modern world and try to make it work better, we have to understand the role of bureaucracy and its purpose. Bureaucracy is one of the ways by which man has sought to muffle the shock-waves of a menacing environment and to establish order in his surroundings. The alternative to bureaucracy is anarchy and injustice—at least in our present stage of human development. A just, ordered society without a bureaucracy has yet to be established. In China Mao Tse-Tung tried to create one with his doctrine of 'permanent revolution', in which the masses would continually overturn the agents of the Establishment, in order to prevent the emergence of a new permanent ruling class as in the USSR, or the return in a new guise of the Confucian-trained Mandarins of Imperial China. Mao has had numerous disciples in the west (including many whose knowledge of his ideas has been highly distorted). But the results in China itself have been hardly conclusive. In the end a bureaucratic apparatus has had to be re-created, to enable the goals of society to be achieved.

Institutional Lag

But of course bureaucracies can vary enormously, in their efficiency, their degree of remoteness from the people, their freedom from graft and corruption, their adherence .to democratic or totalitarian systems, their vitality, speed of decision-making, and so on. On the whole, the greater the pace of change to which they have to accommodate, the more difficult it is for bureaucracies, or for the representative institutions which in democratic systems they exist to serve, to function efficiently; for the essence of institutions, whether bureaucratic or representative, is that they reach decisions slowly. The history of western society in the last century is one of constantly accelerating technological changes, bringing in their wake profound mutations in culture and attitudes, to which bureaucracies and representative institutions have responded with increasing difficulty, with increasing signs of 'institutional lag'. This book has described one part of this process. Other examples in other fields could have been quoted—for example, the effects on international relations and on the human psyche of the invention of the hydrogen bomb, or of the changes in world population due to the discoveries of medical science (some of the results of which will concern us in the next chapter).

The point to be made here is that mankind's ability to absorb change is limited, both individually and institutionally. The American writer Alvin Toffler has described the effects of 'future shock' on people subjected to a faster rate of change than they can accept; and 'future shock' can affect institutions at least as seriously as individuals—especially institutions like bureaucracies which operate according to established rules and criteria which are hard to change, or like representative assemblies where the majority who feel threatened by change can outvote the creative minority who are psychologically conditioned to see the opportunities and to respond positively to them.

In this kind of situation, institutions can become extremely resistant to change; and when this happens, society enters a dangerous phase. Change brought about by technology cannot be ignored, nor can its pace be controlled; but the effects can be distorted by institutional inertia or resistance. The introduction of a new labour-saving technique can be frustrated by legislation, or by trade union insistence on manning levels which make it uneconomic. In this case the technique will be introduced in a foreign country and its products in due course imported, to the cost of the home industry and eventually to jobs. Governments can try to block out unwelcome ideas from abroad, by banning the sale of books or articles containing them. The people will pick them up anyhow, by the circulation of clandestine manuscripts or microfilm, or simply by listening to the foreign radio; the authorities' attempts to suppress them will simply give them greater subversive power.

My contention is that the nation-state in all western countries is to a greater or lesser extent suffering from 'future shock', brought about by the increasing difficulty of absorbing shock waves of change due to autonomous technological advance. That process has been greatly intensified by the breakdown of the Keynesian world order, under the impact of inflationary pressures generated by an upsurge of expectations and the erosion of fatalism among western peoples. The result has been a decline in the quality of decision-making and in the sense of national purpose and social cohesion. The State has tried to take on responsibilities which it cannot meet, and to cling to powers which it can no longer effectively exercise. This has led to a loss of morale, to confusion and conflict. The old sources of cohesion and stability in society—the family, the Church, the local community, the force of custom and tradition—have either disappeared or are seriously weakened. The bureaucracy of the nation-state has not succeeded in replacing them. Consequently there is a growing tendency for people to *opt out*—to seek the solution to their problems in small groups outside the political machine, which can give them the resources or the protection they need, at the expense of the rest of the community; or else to *drop out* of society, and the responsibilities of citizenship, altogether.

The ultimate stage of this process of social breakdown is the Mafia State, where competing gangs wage civil war, where the rich buy protection and security from private organisations, where justice is for sale, and the divorce between power and morality is total. It is the return to Hobbes' nightmare state of nature, from which the Leviathan of the nation-state with its attendant bureaucracy was to rescue us. In certain parts of the modern world we can already see glimpses of this return, and of the kind of future which could be in store for all of us. We only have to watch the television programmes on Northern Ireland, or walk (if we are suicidal enough to do so) in the black quarters of New York, Detroit or Washington. We need only contemplate the growing incidence of kidnapping,[4] hijacks and large-scale crime, as well as the less dramatic but nevertheless significant increase in football hooliganism, vandalism and muggings. We can note, in passing, the rapid expansion of private security organisations, whose job is to protect private property (a task for which the police force was once thought adequate), but which in slightly different circumstances could easily become the nucleus for private armies like the *condottieri* of Renaissance Italy, selling their services to the highest bidder.[5]

We cannot afford to say, 'It can't happen here'. It can, and it may. The fabric of modern society is no more immune from decay than were its predecessors, and the forces of decay are strong. In these circumstances one has to ask oneself whether we can continue any longer with safety along the path trodden during the last century—a path which has led us into a world dominated by huge, alien organisations, a relentless yet unsatisfying pursuit of economic growth at all costs, the proliferation of frightening new technological forces and processes whose end-result we cannot control. Is it not this which has brought us to the situation we now face—the threat of social breakdown and the collapse of our civilisation? Should we not, in face of this danger, try to reorder our priorities and envisage a radical re-structuring of our socio-economic system?

Before we answer this question, we need to look briefly at the world environment within which our threatened western civilisation exists. Is there anything 'out there' which can alter our perspective—for good or, unhappily more likely, for ill?

NOTES TO CHAPTER 5

[1] If present western society can truly be described as 'capitalist'—which, if one follows the argument of this book, is open to question.

[2] The East European countries embrace an increasingly wide spectrum between relative economic liberalism, as in Hungary, albeit within an authoritarian political framework, and the more traditional 'command' economies. One may contrast the relative economic success of post-1956 Hungary with the relative failure of post-1956 Poland.

[3] It is interesting that some of the most successful European societies in the post-war period, such as West Germany and Switzerland, have federal structures of government, with very considerable powers devolved to the regions (*Länder* in Germany, cantons in Switzerland). Internal political stresses are pushing other European countries—Belgium, the UK, Spain and Italy—in the same direction. Outside Europe, the USA, Canada and Australia have had a not unsuccessful experience of federal government—though in Canada Quebec separatism could yet pull the federation apart.

[4] It is surely no coincidence that it should be in Italy, where the reputation and effectiveness of government are lower than in any other western European country, and where economic and social disintegration has proceeded furthest, that kidnapping and extortion should have emerged most markedly as an organised commercial activity. Other states in an apparently advanced stage of social decay, where kidnapping (for commercial or political purposes) is a well-organised growth industry, include the failed democracies of Argentina and Uruguay. Here we see examples of the Mafia State in embryo. Doubtless the techniques of terror, counter-terror and protection which we can see in operation there today will be refined with further experience. Practice, in these as in other matters, makes perfect.

[5] The costs of maintaining law and order are by no means light. Leaving aside the upkeep of the police and judicial systems, it costs today £4,000 to maintain each prisoner per annum. If one adds to this the social security cost of maintaining his dependents, the loss to the economy of the prisoner's labour, the cost of compensating his victims, etc., it becomes clear that the economic burden on the community of social deviance is far from negligible. Prevention can be cheaper than retribution.

6

Expanding, or Exploding, World?

Economically, the world is divided into two main groups. On the one hand, there is the minority group of countries which have been through the industrial revolution, and have acquired industrial systems with the capacity for self-sustaining growth. Most of these countries operate variants of the free-enterprise capitalist system, but a significant minority fall within the Communist camp. On the other hand, there is the majority group of countries which do not have developed industrial economies capable of autonomous growth. Most of the countries in the first group are rich, most of those in the second group very poor. There is a relatively small group of extremely rich but industrially under-developed countries, consisting mainly of the oil exporters. The political and economic systems of the second group of nations vary enormously. A few of them are liberal democracies, a few (notably China) are Communist, most are run by dictators or oligarchies.

Despite all the changes which have occurred in the world in the past fifty years, remarkably few countries have moved from the second group to the first. Those that have are located either in the Sino-Japanese area (Korea, Singapore, Taiwan, Hong Kong), or in Latin America (Brazil—but in the same part of the world Uruguay, Chile and Argentina have arguably dropped from Group One to Group Two, through failure to adapt to some of the pressures described earlier in this book), or the Mediterranean fringe of the European Community. Only one country, Israel, has made the transition while retaining throughout an indisputably democratic system.

The process of industrialisation and economic development

seems a complex one, involving a large number of social and cultural variables. There has to be a social infrastructure which can provide an educated class of managers and bureaucrats, and suffic-ient political, and social stability to enable capital to be accumu-lated. The social climate has to be such that capitalists are encouraged to put their wealth into productive enterprises, rather than into land, jewellery, political bribes or charity. The capital for development may come from private individuals, the State or foreign enterprises or institutions—or, more probably, from a mixture of all these. The critical variable is not the original supply of capital, but the environment in which it is allowed to operate.

The relationship between the two groups of nations is crucial in determining the future growth and stability of the world's politico-economic system. The rich, industrialised group of countries cannot ignore the poor 'third world' (the 'first world' being the western, the 'second world' the Soviet, bloc) countries. It needs their markets to provide an outlet for its surplus manu-factures and its capital. It buys many of its commodities from them. Politically, it cannot afford to see too many of these coun-tries move into the Soviet orbit, and thus swing the world balance of power against the west. Many of the west's large multinational companies have substantial operations in the 'third world'.

The architects of the Keynesian world order after 1945 created a number of institutions, including notably the International Bank for Reconstruction and Development (the 'World Bank'), to channel investment capital from the first to the third world, with the aim of raising living standards and helping the countries con-cerned to achieve self-sustaining economic growth on the western model. In subsequent years major programmes of overseas aid for the less developed countries were mounted by the US, the western European countries, the USSR (and, very recently, the OPEC group of nations).

The results have generally been disappointing. As already in-dicated, the number of developing countries to move into a condition of self-sustaining growth has been very small. Many totally lack the kind of infrastructure which would make such a process possible. But a number of other factors have worked against a greater equalisation of economic wealth, and have instead produced a growing world polarisation between rich and poor countries.

One such factor has been the impact of western technology, which has greatly increased the productivity of western food production and has increasingly found synthetic substitutes for natural materials. This has reduced the demand in the west for the raw materials, whether metals, foodstuffs, textiles or other commodities, which were previously supplied by the third world, below what one might otherwise have expected. With certain significant exceptions—of which oil is the outstanding example— the terms of trade have moved to the disadvantage of the third world and in favour of the industrialised west in the last two decades. The western countries have ceased to be major net food importers in a number of instances, and in certain areas they have become significant exporters of food to the third world. Moreover, where the third world has established itself as a low-cost manufacturer (as, for example, in clothing and textiles) seeking to export to the west on the basis of low labour costs, western trade unions have tried to limit such imports in order to protect their members' jobs. Governments have not always resisted this pressure.

Thus the balance of trade and investment between the first and third worlds has been disturbed. The old order, under which the west exported capital and manufactures to the third world in exchange for raw materials and food, is no longer viable. Any new economic order would need to provide western outlets for low-cost, low-technology manufactures from the third world, to offset the relatively declining western demand for food and raw materials. But this the west finds hard to accept at a time of high and persistent unemployment.

Meanwhile the third world is heavily in debt to the first world as a result of the heavy capital investment undertaken in the last two decades. Unless the debts can be re-scheduled or written off, the third world (excluding the OPEC countries) will be transferring capital to the first world during the next decade. Both sides are acutely dissatisfied with the results which this investment has achieved. The western countries claim (and there is little doubt that the Soviet bloc investors feel also) that much of the aid given, and the capital lent, has been wastefully used. The third world replies that the industrialised countries have equipped it with technologies that are inappropriate, because they are over-sophisticated and designed to save labour, which is one resource which the third world has in abundance; that in their aid and investment programmes they have failed to study and respond to the needs and circumstances of the recipients, but have instead considered only the convenience of the suppliers; that multinational companies, with the connivance of western governments, have exploited the third world countries where they operate; that the west has artificially depressed the market for third world commodities, and restricted the import of third world food and manufactures for the benefit of higher-cost domestic suppliers; and so on. A new world economic order must correct these injustices and anomalies, if the rich are not to get richer and the poor poorer, with all the attendant strains and dangers for the entire planet.

Rising Tensions in the Third World

Behind this increasingly tense debate lie two enormously important facts about the third world. The first is the increase of expectations among its people. We have referred to this phenomenon, and its revolutionary consequences, in the countries of the industrialised west. But the 'revolt of the masses' (to use the phrase coined by the Spanish writer Ortega y Gasset) has spread to the people of the third world also, for the same reasons.[1]

The second factor which has revolutionised the position of the third world has been the explosion of world population, resulting from medical technology. At present the world's population—currently just over 4,000 million—is doubling approximately every thirty-five years. This means that on present trends, there will be 8,000 million people on this planet by the year 2010 (eight times as many as a hundred years ago). The great bulk of this increase is taking place in the developing countries. The rich industrial countries are able to limit their population growth by planned contraception, but this is beyond the means—in most cases, outside the knowledge—of the great majority of people in the third world.

It is this explosive growth in population which has widened the gap in living standards between the rich and the poor countries. It has increased enormously the demand for food in the third world, thus reducing the net surplus available for export. It has meant that the increased output generated by industrial investment has to be shared among more and more people, so that output per head of population has in some cases actually declined in the last ten years among the developing countries. Finally, it has produced a massive movement of people from the countryside into the cities of the third world, in search of a livelihood which the villages cannot provide. (Most of the aid for the third world has gone into urban rather than rural projects.) Unfortunately, few of the third world's cities are equipped to absorb the massive influx of people which they have been experiencing, whether in terms of jobs available for them or of an infrastructure to support them. In the cities the poor are as badly off as they were in the villages, but they are made more aware of the gap between themselves and the rich, they become more bitter and alienated, and the explosive potential in the countries concerned grows with the spread of urbanisation. Misery and poverty, which can remain hidden and inert in the countryside, become visible and vocal in the urban slums.

The population explosion may indeed be having even more sinister effects on society, both in the developing and the developed countries. There is an alarming body of evidence to suggest that an excessive concentration of population in a given territory produces recognisable stress symptoms in most kinds of mammals, including man, leading to irrational and hysterical behaviour, violence, and withdrawal symptoms. If this condition exists, the

nature of modern urban life—the noise, the traffic, the bombard-
ment of the mass media, the juxtaposition of extreme wealth and
poverty, the pressure on housing, the absorption of alien minorities—would certainly intensify it. It may be that we need to
introduce stringent population control not just to conserve resources, or to reduce economic disparities between the rich and
poor countries, but to preserve the mental and psychological
health of the species. However, whichever way one looks at it, the
problem of surplus and exploding population hits the third world
countries with special severity.

And so the dialogue between rich nations and poor grows more
tense and strident, as the governments of the poor countries become more and more conscious of the powder-keg on which they
are sitting. The problems of the internal dialogue between the
social groups within the western industrial countries are mirrored
and magnified in the controversy between rich and poor countries on the world stage. In their bitterness and frustration, the
third world nations are increasingly tending to seek control over
the foreign investors—essentially the multinational companies—
operating in their territories. These measures tend to frighten the
investors, with the result that the flow of western capital is falling
off just when it is most needed. Many of the specific complaints
made about the pattern of past western investment in the third
world are true. But the west, the main source of capital for development and the major market for the third world's products, still has
most of the bargaining cards in its hands. The third world has to
persuade the west to adopt a more co-operative posture; it cannot
compel it to do so. In the western world the balance of domestic
power has moved, in large measure, from the elites to the masses.
But on the world stage it is still the rich nations which wield the
power.

So the power groups in the developing countries occupy a very
exposed position. The masses grow more and more restive, the
western nations seem less and less able or willing to give aid on the
scale needed. Inflation has hit the third world as it has the first
world; but the poor in the third world are much less able than

their fellows in the west to cope with higher prices. It is not surprising that the small minority of genuine democracies among the third world countries has shrunk even further in the 1970s (losing, significantly, India[2] and Bangladesh, as well as a number of Latin American countries); in contrast, as we have seen, to the trend in Europe.

Whether or not it will be possible to construct a more satisfactory world economic order, unless and until the west solves its own internal problems, is hard to predict. In the meantime one thing is clear. The problems which we have been discussing in this book, as a phenomenon of contemporary western society, are mirrored on an expanded scale on the world scene. The world is becoming a more unequal, and a more dangerous, place. People everywhere are becoming more conscious of inequalities, and more resentful of their effects. The *expanding* world economy which emerged from the Second World War, in which wealth would gradually filter out from the rich countries to the poor, through trade and capital flows buttressed by aid, has turned into an *exploding* world, in which population grows faster in the poor countries than the means to feed, house or employ them, where the return on capital invested in these countries is judged unsatisfactory for different reasons by both supplier and user, and where the flows of both capital and trade have become distorted. If this dangerous situation is to be defused, two things have to happen. Measures to contain population growth in the third world have to be intensified; and the west has to put its own house in order, so that it can play a useful part in re-structuring the Keynesian world order which has fallen apart, on the world as on the domestic scene. How is this to be done?

NOTES TO CHAPTER 6

[1] 'Masses' is perhaps a somewhat ambiguous term in the third world context. The transmitters of discontent have tended to be educated, or at least semi-educated, elites who have had the opportunity of access to western ideas and have communicated their rising expectations to others. But of course there is

nothing very new in this. Revolutions are normally made, not by the starving, but by the relatively well-to-do. This does not make the grievances any less real. And the nature of events is continually widening the circle of those whose expectations have been aroused but unsatisfied.

[2] Happily, since this was written, India has returned to the ranks of parliamentary democracy. But for how long?

7
Alternative Solutions

When things have reached the pass indicated in the preceding chapters, it is hardly surprising that people are prepared to envisage radical alternatives. Many such have been proposed in the last few years, which, if adopted, would involve fundamental changes to the western socio-economic system.

One of the most powerful movements of ideas during the 1970s has been the attack, orchestrated by the Club of Rome but supported by a number of independent economists (E. J. Mishan is a prominent British example), ecologists, scientists and sociologists, on the whole concept of economic growth as a social objective. In its highly influential book, *The Limits to Growth*, the Club of Rome produced an economic model which purported to prove that economic growth would sooner or later run up against insurmountable bottlenecks arising from pollution, unsustainable population growth, and shortages of non-renewable materials. Consequently it would be necessary, if western society was to survive, to reorder our priorities, giving a much lower priority to the proliferation of consumer goods, and concentrating rather on the 'recycling' of materials, conservation and protection of the environment, and the establishment and maintenance of a 'stable state' economy.[1]

A number of points need to be made about this thesis. First, it is undeniable that the explosive growth in world population poses one of the greatest challenges to the future stability of society, and that population control is an urgent priority over most of the globe. But it is not clear what the connection is between *population* growth and *economic* growth. The Club of Rome and its supporters sometimes seem to argue as if the latter in some way *caused* the former. It is hard to see how such a causal relation could be substantiated. What is much more plausible is that population growth both *stimulates* economic growth, by providing an expanding market and an expanding labour force, and *requires* it, by creating new material needs (including the need for jobs). Thus the growth in population seems, other things equal, to provide an argument for the maintenance of high rates of economic growth rather than the opposite.

Can We Afford Growth?

But *are* other things equal? Does the world have the resources to sustain a continuation of the rates of economic growth achieved since 1945? This is the second line of argument of the 'zero growth' school, and it is as old as the beginning of the industrial revolution, when it was advanced by the English economist Thomas Malthus. The fact that Malthusian arguments have been consistently disproved by events so far does not mean that they can be ignored today. On the other hand, the development of large food surpluses in the industrialised countries, and the growth of synthetic substitutes for natural raw materials, which we noted in the last chapter, does seem to suggest that the era of exhaustion of materials may be a little way off, to put it mildly.

In fact, there are two main critical areas. The first is *food*. With the world population doubling every thirty-five years or so, the problem of food supplies is bound to be critical. In fact, the evidence suggests that the use of fertilisers and modern farming methods can produce, in the third world as it has in the west, enormous increases in agricultural productivity. And there are vast potential sources of food production as yet untapped, such as the development of large-scale commercial fish farming, or of synthetic food protein (likely to move into large-scale commercial exploitation by the early 1980s). The problem is not likely to be the adequacy of food resources, but the difficulties of distribution, and the side-effects of the necessary changes in agricultural technology.

For example, how are the food surpluses in the rich countries to be distributed to the poor in the third world who need them? Are transport systems in the developing countries adequate to deliver the food to the remoter areas? How will the third world countries pay for the imports of food, and of food technology, likely to be needed? What are likely to be the ecological effects of intensive agricultural production, and the large-scale use of fertilisers and insecticides? And what about the social effects—if, as seems likely, more effective land-use requires the kind of transition from peasant to capitalist farming which has been taking place in Europe?

In other words, there *are* serious issues involved in feeding the world's burgeoning population, but they are issues of economic, political and social organisation, and of the quality of the world's environment. The problems are by no means technically insoluble, but solving them will raise difficult value-choices about the kind of world we want to live in.

The question turns out to be very similar when we look at other raw materials. In every case the evidence suggests that ample reserves are likely to be available, and/or that synthetic substitutes can be developed. But some of the substitutes have heavy environmental risks—to health, safety or ecology—and tapping the reserves available will certainly involve substantial extra costs (many of them for example lie on or under the bed of the oceans which cover 70% of the earth's surface).

The position can be demonstrated by examining the second critical area on which the 'zero-growth' school concentrates its attack—sources of *energy*. This is one area where the demand for non-renewable resources is directly related to the requirements of industrial growth. At present there is a world energy shortage, which explains the remarkable success of the OPEC countries in jacking up world prices. The supply of fossil fuels (oil, natural gas, coal, lignite, peat) from existing known reserves is, by definition, limited; and if one thinks only in terms of these reserves the possibility of exhaustion, with all the implications for the future of the world's economy, has to be taken very seriously.

But is this a realistic approach? The pace of exploration for fossil fuels has been stepped up enormously as a reaction to the present dominance of the market by the OPEC cartel, and a remarkable number of new reserves both of oil and coal have been discovered. The problem is much more likely to be one of cost of extraction— once again, many of the newly-discovered fields are offshore (like the North Sea) or in remote, inaccessible places (like the Alaskan and Canadian Arctic)—and of possible ecological damage, than lack of physical availability.

Moreover, there are known alternative sources of energy to the fossil fuels—ranging from relatively futuristic (but technically feasible) methods like the harnessing of solar or tidal energy, to the most important immediate alternative, nuclear energy. Nuclear energy has been handicapped up to now by its high cost in relation to fossil fuels. Now, however, the cost differential is narrowing, and the nuclear option looks much more attractive— in economic terms; especially with the development of man-made plutonium as the basic material in place of the much rarer natural metal, uranium.

The nuclear debate focuses today on a different issue. The question at stake is whether a plutonium-based energy economy poses acceptable risks to society. These risks are of many kinds. There is the danger of an accidental explosion—which could be caused by a natural hazard, like an earth tremor—or of a 'leak' of radio-activity (there is the problem of the safe disposal of radio-active waste from the power stations). There is the argument that possession of plutonium gives a country the ability to manufacture nuclear weapons. Any country which has a nuclear power station on its territory has the capacity to make its own atomic arms; how in these circumstances can one prevent the proliferation of nuclear weaponry, with the attendant risks to world peace? Finally, there is the nightmare prospect that a gang of terrorists or criminals might raid a nuclear power station, seize a supply of plutonium, and use it to blackmail the country concerned into meeting its demands.

In short, the argument about energy boils down to questions about the costs we are prepared to pay, and the risks we are prepared to run, in order to assure ourselves of adequate resources to fuel an expanding economy. The choices are agonisingly difficult, but it looks as if we can have continued growth *at a price*. The question is whether the price is worth paying.

Pollution: Physical and Social

The issue turns out to be the same when we examine the third of the Club of Rome's constraints to growth, pollution. There is no doubt that much harm has been done to the earth's environment during the great Keynesian industrial boom. Non-disposable wastes, some of them toxic, have disfigured the landscape, and (more seriously) damaged the ecological balance in some of the world's lakes and rivers. Some industrial materials have turned out, unexpectedly, to be serious health hazards. The quality of urban living has been damaged by excessive noise levels, the smog brought about by car exhausts, and other by-products of industrial affluence.

But, despite various scare stories put out during the last few years (such as the imminent destruction of the ozone by indiscriminate use of aerosols, or irreversible changes to the climate due to pollution of the atmosphere by industrial emissions), the balance of objective scientific evidence suggests that no irretrievable damage to the physical environment has yet been done. Thus pollution is no more an absolute barrier to future economic growth than is material shortage. But, as with material shortage, the avoidance of future pollution, and the rectifying of the damage done by past and present pollution, will involve extra costs to society and some difficult choices as to future priorities.

Thus what the growth debate appears to show is not that western society is faced with a categorical imperative, to abandon the pursuit of growth or face certain disaster, but rather that we have to consider a series of very difficult choices, as to the other values we are prepared to sacrifice for growth, the costs we are prepared to incur to maintain it, and the risks we are ready to face. The question boils down to one of social priorities.

This becomes very clear when one examines the arguments of some of the more eloquent members of the 'anti-growth' school outside the Club of Rome, such as E. J. Mishan. Mishan and his supporters base their argument, not so much on the objective dangers of a continuing high rate of growth, as on the claim that such growth on present evidence fails to make people happier, but on the contrary lowers the quality of life. The argument is thus explicitly based on subjective value-judgements—dangerous ground, one might think, for an economist to occupy.

Mishan and his school nevertheless mount a persuasive attack on the harm which excessive concentration on economic growth has allegedly done. Growth has raised expectations which it is incapable of satisfying (an argument which we have advanced in this book); it has made people greedy and materialistic, and militated against equality and comradeship; it has lowered the quality of life in cities, and damaged the amenities of the countryside; it has exposed us to the risks of pollution, and also to the possibilities of political manipulation through electronic developments (the invasion of privacy by computer data-storage, and by electronic 'bugging' devices). All of these ills have fallen upon us, or threaten us, because of our insane urge for greater and greater material wealth.

I hope that I have given a fair, if telescoped, summary of the 'anti-growth' arguments. (I should add that in its later writings the Club of Rome has moved some way beyond the rather crude *simpliste*, pseudo-quantifiable arguments of *The Limits to Growth*.) I believe the balance of evidence indicates that there are as yet *no* discernible *absolute* limits to growth; on the other hand, the Club of Rome and its supporters have performed a valuable service to mankind in indicating, more clearly than ever before, some of the social costs of the particular growth pattern which the industrial world has hitherto followed. There seems to me an undeniable argument in favour of inducing certain changes in the growth pattern for the future.

Thus, for example, industrial polluters should be expected to pay the social costs of the pollution they cause, and this should be incorporated in the cost of the product. The 'anti-growth' school sometimes argue as if industrial pollution was something new. But nobody who has seen the slagheaps and debris left by the nineteenth-century coal-based industrial economy could fall into this error. In most respects the factories of the present day are vastly more acceptable ecologically than their predecessors. But it is clearly right that the closest watch should be kept on any signs of industrial damage to the environment, and that the polluter (and ultimately the consumer of his product) should be made responsible for rectifying any such damage.

Similarly, there is everything to be said for incentives to promote energy-saving and the 'recycling' of materials. A high priority should be given, for example, to the development of electrically-powered cars, to replace the polluting (and increasingly expensive) internal combustion engine. Many other examples could be given. The point is that the evils of pollution can and should be rectified, through the use of the price mechanism, aided by judicious use of government incentives and deterrents (via the tax system, allocation of public research and development funds, and controls). In this way the productive system can be made more socially responsible, and resources within it re-allocated to modify the growth pattern into more acceptable forms.

This is unlikely to satisfy the radical exponents of the 'anti-growth' school, who argue that nothing short of a total re-ordering of our priorities away from growth and towards maintenance of a 'stable state' situation is going to solve our problems. I find this argument unpersuasive. The argument seems in some areas to confuse cause and effect. It is not the process of growth which has aroused expectations. It is rather the demand for better living standards which has called forth the growth. We saw in earlier chapters that the present inflation arises primarily because the demands being placed on the productive system have outshot its ability to meet them. It does not seem, therefore, that present social tensions are going to be eased, or people made happier, by deliberately restricting output even below the inadequate (in relation to demand) performance of which it is technologically capable—unless at the same time one can so educate the mass of the populace that they will cease to demand the goods and services for which they clamour so insistently today.[2]

It may be unfortunate for the middle classes that the masses are demanding the kind of life-style which has hitherto been reserved for the elite, and in so doing making it increasingly unattractive. (The idyllic holiday retreat loses its charm once it gets onto the coach tour circuit.) One can sympathise over the loss of amenities which depend for their value on their exclusivity. There is no doubt that the more affluent people are, the more mobility they crave, and therefore the more land-space they occupy (and land is the one basic economic resource whose supply is ultimately in-elastic). But by what moral, let alone economic, criterion can one justify the exclusion of the masses from the privileges enjoyed by a few?[3]

Much of the writing of the 'anti-growth' school has the senti-mental flavour of yearning for a lost pre-industrial Arcadia, a return to the unchanging values of a static society. It echoes the elitist arguments of a Matthew Arnold, lamenting the philistinism of an egalitarian culture. The proletariat have bought entrance tickets to the Garden of Eden, and once inside they are picking the flowers and trampling over the grass. Certain economic goods lose their value if they become too widely distributed, since part of this value rests in exclusivity, in the advantages or prestige which ownership of them brings. What is the point of having a mink coat or a Jaguar XJS, if everybody else has one? Similarly, a university degree may give one a head-start in getting a good job, but not if too many other people have one also. So, in a real sense, the distribution of goods over a wider community lessens their relative value to those who already have them, even though the absolute supply is unaffected.

This is a valid, if selfish, argument against economic growth from the point of view of the well-to-do. But what about the majority, for whom the possession of these goods, however tarn-ished, represents a major improvement in their life-style? It may be, human nature being what it is, that human aspirations will never be satisfied, and that the pursuit of greater material wealth will thus never be ultimately rewarding. It may be, as earlier chapters have hinted, that mankind would have been happier had the industrial revolution never happened. That is a question to which we can never know the answer—and anyway, from a practical point of view it is quite irrelevant. For the fact is that the revolution did take place, there is a constantly expanding world population to be fed, clothed, housed and employed, and expectations have been aroused throughout the world which will hardly disappear of their own volition. The population explosion imports its own dynamic into the world economy, making a return to a stable state economy unrealisable. And the revolution of rising expectations also provides a dynamic, for there is nothing more damaging to human happiness or the equilibrium of society than the frustration of hopes.

So the two preconditions for a successful 'zero-growth' economy, it seems to me, must be (a) a stabilisation in world population, and (b) a reversal of aspirations for a better material life-style on the part of the mass of the world's peoples. I see little evidence of either of these preconditions being met in the near future.

A Re-oriented Growth Pattern?

It follows, I believe, that whether we like it or not we are condemned to the treadmill of higher growth for some time to come. The problem, as already indicated, is rather going to be to re-establish and maintain a rate of growth sufficient to satisfy social demands and expectations. But it does not follow that we are condemned to repeat the same pattern of economic development as has been followed since 1945. I have already indicated that we need to switch resources to some extent away from the replication of consumer goods—at least in the richer countries—in favour of more expenditure on 'social' goods such as energy conservation, environmental protection, and aid to the poorer countries. It is how we allocate our resources, it seems to me, that we should be discussing, rather than the essentially arid question of whether we should be aiming to grow our economies at 5% or 2% or zero per annum. I believe there is enough to do in the world to employ all our resources, if only we can allocate them in the most desirable way. And the means for so doing rest essentially with a more purposeful use of the price mechanism by the political authorities—supplemented, where necessary, by legislation and controls.

The argument can be put another way. The real limits to growth, it is being increasingly argued, are not the material ones posited by the Club of Rome in *The Limits to Growth*, but rather *social* constraints, imposed by the unacceptability of the conditions required for further growth, in terms of the damage to the environment and the quality of life, both for the workers producing the growth and the broader community outside. Thus any growth pattern has to come to terms with social aspirations if it is to be politically viable.

The industrial system has always made heavy demands on those working in it, as we saw in Chapter 4. As technology has advanced, the requirement for back-breaking toil has diminished as machines have increasingly replaced human sweat. But there have been offsetting disadvantages. One has been the development of 'Taylorism', the system by which productivity is raised by breaking down the work performed by each operative on a moving production line to the smallest possible number of separate tasks— taking individual specialisation, in short, to the highest degree possible. The psychological result of the application of Taylorism, as educational standards and aspirations have risen in recent years, has been growing resistance to the monotony of the working pattern involved; and so we have seen, as indicated in Chapter 4, a growing tendency to revert to earlier methods of production (albeit with ultra-modern control systems), giving each individual a greater variety of tasks to perform, and a greater autonomy in the way in which he chooses to perform these tasks. An alternative approach has been to automate the work on the assembly line to the point at which the production flow is controlled and carried out by computer-programmed robots in place of human workers.

Monotony has been part of the price extorted by technological innovation in certain sectors of the productive process. Another result has been the necessity for continual change, by managers and workers alike, in the methods and conditions of work, and the skills required. This, too, is generating growing resistance on the part of workers suffering from increasing doses of 'future shock'.

For economic growth to retain acceptability, therefore, it has to be seen to be responding to these demands from the work-force, and also to the requirements of the environment indicated above. The contribution of the productive system to the overall quality of life has to be clear and beyond dispute. Moreover, the fruits of economic growth, as well as the resources to produce it, have to be distributed in a way which commands broad social approval.

The Attack on Leviathan

These principles have a number of implications for the future ordering of society. That the present system is unsatisfactory is common ground among a number of writers who are not necessarily hostile to growth as such. One persistent line of criticism concerns the tendency of both the political and industrial systems to coalesce into large units and highly institutionalised structures. Thus Ivan Illich attacks the growth of large institutions in such fields as education and public health, arguing that people would be better educated and healthier if we had fewer teachers and doctors, and spent less on schools and hospitals. Bureaucracy and institutionalisation, he argues, are killing the spirit of spontaneity and self-reliance. Not only is this happening in the advanced industrial countries, but these countries are exporting the same weaknesses to the third world via their aid programmes.[4]

This essentially anarchistic approach, which attacks both capitalist and Marxist orthodoxy, finds considerable support at both ends of the political spectrum in many countries. On the extreme Left, especially among the students, one finds the disciples of Marcuse and Guevara, who believe in the ultimate goodness of man, once freed from the shackles of exploiting institutions. Only destroy the restrictive apparatus of the State, and you will release the creative instincts of humanity. Liberation is all. On the extreme Right, the attack on the State bureaucracy is mounted, for quite different reasons, by monetarist economists like Milton Friedman. They believe that the State pre-empts too many of the resources of society, and spends them much less effectively than would the individuals from whom they have been taken. They would like to see the State restricting its activities to the maintenance of law and order, control of the money supply, and the redistribution of income through 'negative income tax' systems. The provision of welfare should be left as far as possible to the initiative of individuals and commercial organisations, responding to the pressures of the market (pressures which would, of course, have been influenced by the State's redistribution of purchasing power through the tax system). Business enterprises should eschew all social responsibilities other than maximising profits. In his writings Friedman repeatedly criticises the inflexibility of the 'political market' in the allocation of goods and services, as compared with the commercial market. In the 'political market', if 51% of potential customers vote for a certain allocation, the wishes of the other 49% go unheard. But in the commercial market each individual has some purchasing power, and therefore some influence on the way resources are allocated.

In one sense, the arguments of Illich and Friedman are the lineal descendants of those advanced by Pelagius in the fifth century, and by Locke and Rousseau in the eighteenth. They express the belief—in contrast to St Augustine and Hobbes, for example—that man is basically good, and society therefore, in so far as it seeks to constrain him, is basically evil. For Hobbes, society (and for Augustine, the Church) could make large claims on man—for the state of nature (for Augustine, original sin) was so heinous that even an oppressive society was a better alternative. For Locke and Rousseau, by contrast, the social contract which led men from a relatively blissful state of nature into ordered society had to concede substantial liberties to the individual if it was to justify itself.

Today the relative failures of the State make the case for more individual freedom, whether it is advanced from the Left or the Right, look more than usually persuasive. The problem, however, is not just that the performance of modern society looks poor; it is also that the pursuit of growth has led to a concentration of resources into larger and larger units, more and more remote from the individual whom they are allegedly seeking to serve, and with slower and slower reactions. In the business field Graham Bannock has written scornfully of the 'Juggernauts'—huge, insensitive business corporations whose ability to respond to market pressures diminishes the bigger they grow. E. F. Schumacher has coined the slogan 'Small is Beautiful', to express his rejection of giantism in business enterprises, political systems and institutions generally.

Writers such as Schumacher are also concerned at what they regard as the distortion of technology to serve the behests of the giant institutions of the private and public sector, instead of re-sponding to the real demands of society. Schumacher accuses the west of trying to impose its own technology, geared to the needs of a society where labour is scarce and expensive and capital rela-tively cheap, on a third world where in general exactly the reverse is true. He presses for the development of what he calls *inter-mediate* technology to solve the—often rather small and relatively simple—problems of the developing countries; such technology uses the resources which these countries possess, and does not demand skills and know-how which are beyond them.

Other writers have applied the same kind of argument to the social problems of industrialised societies, arguing for *radical* or *alternative* technologies, which can be applied to the solution of problems without requiring large injections of capital, or the kind of know-how and management which tend, in our society, to be monopolised by large organisations. Such technologies do not start from the proposition, which their proponents argue orthodox technology does in both capitalist and Marxist economies, that technical advance consists of increases in capital intensity, in the scale of operation and the complexity of structures.

What we are seeing here is a reaction, healthy if sometimes exaggerated, against the trend towards mergers and large-scale operations which has characterised the development of industrial society so far. Economic and business theory has made much of the economies of large scale; we are beginning to become painfully aware of the *diseconomies*. The economies are real. Broadly speaking, the longer the production run of a particular product, the lower the unit cost. Thus the large-scale producer can usually undercut his smaller competitor, particularly if he is selling a standard product. Overhead costs become less onerous, the bigger the output against which to offset them. The large-scale producer can usually obtain significant economies in marketing costs, in research and development (R & D), in the deployment of management resources, in purchasing, and so on.

The diseconomies are less easily quantifiable, but none the less important. They focus essentially on the problems of managing large units, avoiding alienation and remoteness, and retaining the capacity to respond swiftly to market changes and to innovate. It is no coincidence that, by and large, labour problems tend to be more intractable in large units. The bad relations are, in a sense, a function of the distance between the top management and the shopfloor. Another problem is the power which concentration in large units gives to small groups of workers occupying key positions in the productive process. (This has long been a feature of manufacturing industry, and it now looks like becoming a feature of public welfare systems as well, for in this sector the State has been following the example of private enterprise and concentrating activities into large units subject to a high degree of union control.)

There is thus a growing tendency in management structures throughout the world to decentralise decision-making, and—wherever technology permits—to divide operations among a number of relatively small, discrete units. This trend towards *operational decentralisation* is of course entirely compatible with a continuing trend towards *financial centralisation*, as the pressure of competition strengthens the relative position of multinational and/or multi-product companies, which can play individual markets off against each other, using strength in one area to support another. The tendency is for the average size and complexity of enterprises to grow, but for each enterprise to devolve authority internally—partly for ease of management control (so that each manager has a manageable span of responsibility), partly to help to humanise the productive process (by restricting internal bureaucracy), partly to prevent the growth of shopfloor counter-vailing power (by dividing the work-force among a large number of separate locations).

This trend has been facilitated by recent changes in the economic structure of the main industrialised countries. In all these countries the share of the total labour force employed in primary and manufacturing industry is declining relative to that employed in the service sector. Some authorities, such as the American Herman Kahn, have described western society as a 'post-industrial society', though 'post-manufacturing' would be a more accurate term. The growing service sector of the western economy is a very mixed one. A large part, as we have seen, is in the public domain, operating outside the market sector of the economy in what are basically non-productive areas. But another large, and rapidly growing, element consists either of services to industry or services catering to an increasingly affluent consumer market (leisure, entertainment, travel, etc.). A common feature of many of the operations in this private sector services field is that the basic resource is knowledge and its exploitation.

Thus, for example, the development of computer-based information storage and retrieval systems has revolutionised control and communications systems in industry, and has created a rapidly growing industry in its own right. The transmission of know-how and techniques by consultant firms is a growing feature of the business scene in all advanced industrial countries. In a world of affluent consumers the ability to create new tastes and new markets by creativity in design, sales promotion and product development is a surer way to profits than the ability to mass-produce on large-scale assembly lines.

Knowledge-based industries—and in this sector, unlike basic manufacturing, the advanced industrial countries are likely to retain their competitive advantage over the third world for some time to come—require a different structure and a different ethos from the large-scale capital-intensive manufacturing industries which until recently employed the bulk of the labour force in western society. Their basic resource is extremely mobile. Thus it needs to be allowed to operate in congenial and stimulating surroundings, and the business climate needs to be permissive and participative if the knowledge-workers are to be productive and creative. The economies of large scale in such a business are relatively few. Thus in this growing sector of western business society the 'small-is-beautiful' thesis demonstrably works.

However, the absorption of many of their ideas into a social structure which is still basically oriented towards the maximisation of economic growth, however defined, will not satisfy the radical critics of our society, who argue that growth and profits must be subordinated as objectives to other aims—improved quality of life, service to the community, self-sufficiency, renewal and protection of the environment, and so on. The basic question posed in this chapter cannot be evaded. Can a profit-and-growth-oriented society adequately meet these other, clearly desirable, objectives, or not? In other words, can the Keynesian system be reformed, or must it be abandoned? How radical are the changes needed if western civilisation is to survive?[5]

The radical alternatives share one common factor. They require a general willingness on the part of the people in western society to accept fundamental changes in life-style. They require a reversal of the desire, so manifest over the last decade, to accumulate more and more consumer goods and to secure an ever-rising living standard, expressed in currently conventional terms. They require the subordination of materialism to other ideals.

Here and there in the western world one finds communities of people who are prepared to turn their back on the materialist way of life. 'Hippy' communes, 'flower-people', 'good-lifers' and others have been prepared to follow the life of fraternal austerity pioneered in the heyday of Christianity by the orders of monks and friars. But in the broad mass of western society they constitute a small, freakish minority. There is little or no evidence of a religious revival, or a cult of austerity, which would be strong enough to replace the strident emphasis of a materialist culture, propagated by mass media of a strength and sophistication hitherto unknown. Nor does there seem to be any way in which the media could be induced, persuaded or forced to reverse the messages which they have up to now been transmitting, and concentrate on preaching austerity and self-abnegation in place of material betterment.

We live, whether we like it or not, in a post-religious era, and the vacuum left by religion has been filled by a kind of humanistic materialism. The radical critics of our society do well to warn us of the dangers, and are fully entitled to try to persuade us to adopt alternative life-styles. They are not entitled, on the best scientific evidence so far available, to tell us that if we continue on the present path our planet is doomed to extinction, or civilisation in its present form to total and inevitable collapse. The prospect is not quite as black as the 'doom-watchers' suggest. But the risks ahead are certainly very formidable, and it would be good if more people were to heed the warnings which the Club of Rome and others have been sounding, and nerve themselves to modify the socio-economic system to meet the more immediate threats.

But it is one thing to make modifications in the existing system; it is quite another to change it totally in the direction called for by the radical reformers, replacing growth and profits by quite different objectives. Such a change would not, it seems to me, conform to the present wishes of the great majority of western people. If one could be as sure as the Club of Rome that conforming to these wishes will lead us to certain disaster, one would be entitled to use any means to change the course of society. But if, as seems to me to be the case (on present knowledge), what we are arguing about is not survival but the quality of life, it behoves us to be cautious about imposing our subjective preference in life-styles on our fellows. We should argue and seek to influence; we are not entitled to use compulsion, unless basic issues of health and safety are at stake.

I believe, therefore, that we have to concentrate on trying to find ways of making the existing system work better, in terms of meeting the demands of our people, of raising the quality of life, and of protecting the environment. This can only be done, given the present disparity between demands on the productive system and its performance, by trying to achieve the optimum rate *and pattern* of economic growth. How is this to be done, and how are we to secure a social climate in which the productive system can be allowed to operate in such a way as to meet these three fundamental objectives?

NOTES TO CHAPTER 7

[1] I do not want to give the impression that the Club of Rome have patent rights on the 'stable-state' approach. The concept has been explored by many economists, notably in the U S, e.g. Professors Herman Daly and Kenneth Boulding.

[2] I should stress, in fairness to the Club of Rome and other advocates of the 'stable state', that their theses are not designed as answers to the inflation problem, but to solve what they regard as otherwise insoluble problems of material (especially energy) shortages and pollution. The debate on growth was launched before inflation emerged as (in my view) the west's gravest economic problem. My argument in this book is that acceptance of the 'stable state' approach would worsen the inflation problem, and that the other ills to which they address themselves can be solved by other means.

[3] This case can lead us into rather abstruse realms of welfare economics. It would be open to Dr Mishan to argue that the masses *cannot* enjoy the privileges of the few because wider accessibility destroys them altogether. In other words, it is either a few or none at all! To this I would reply that the value of a privilege does not disappear suddenly; it becomes steadily diluted as more and more people enjoy it; in other words, the enjoyment is spread more thinly over a widening circle of people, until eventually it may become diluted to vanishing point. At what point in this process do the welfare *disbenefits* of the dilution of enjoyment for each individual recipient offset the welfare *benefits* for the increased numbers of recipients—bearing in mind that the calculus must involve posterity as well as the present generation? (If the reader feels the argument verges on unreality he has my sympathy!). This whole subject, incidentally, is brilliantly dealt with by Fred Hirsch in his book, *Social Limits to Growth* (Routledge & Kegan Paul, 1977).

[4] This very brief reference does less than justice to the subtlety and perception of Illich's attack on conventional approaches to schooling and medicine. On

the former, he directs his attack on the role of educational establishments in propagating orthodoxies which may be already out-of-date, irrelevant or disproven, and discouraging individual intellectual exploration. On medicine, he points to the deleterious side-effects which too many drugs and other medical treatments have, so that in curing one disease doctors are too often simply easing the path for another. Even when they succeed in improving physical health, this may simply be at the cost of weakening resistance to psycho-somatic ailments. In short, doctors too often are trained to treat particular symptoms, and not to look at the 'whole man'.

Clearly this attack is not without force. But sometimes Illich and his supporters press their case too hard. It is true that we all have to die some time, and therefore if fewer people die of one cause, more are likely to die of another. But not all causes of death or diseases are equal. Some are a good deal nastier than others; they kill more people, more painfully, at an earlier age. The fact that people are living longer indicates that medical technology is not entirely useless. The fact that many of us live unhealthy lives—eating, drinking and smoking too much, taking too little exercise, absorbing too many noxious substances from the environment, and subject to too much stress at work—is not primarily the fault of the medical profession.

5 It may seem perverse that in this chapter devoted to alternative solutions to the present socio-economic problems of the west, I do not consider the obvious alternative posed by Marxist socialism. My excuse is that, as I tried to argue in Chapter 5, the Marxist systems in force in the USSR and Eastern Europe exhibit many if not all the ills currently seen in the west, as well as some special ones of their own. The schools of thought surveyed in this chapter are without exception as unacceptable to, and as hostile towards, the Soviet system as they are to western capitalism. Both socialism and capitalism seek to maximise economic growth. Socialist systems appear less concerned with the consumer, less sensitive to environmental damage, more ready to disrupt traditional social patterns in the cause of 'social engineering', than the neo-capitalist societies of the west. Their pursuit of producer interests is more single-minded, their objectives more limited and materialist, their capacity for self-criticism and internal change vastly less. I do not believe, therefore, that for the ills diagnosed in this book socialism à la russe offers a plausible cure. There are of course other possible variants of socialism. Socialism à la Chinoise, though plainly still in process of evolution, may offer an attractive option for third world—though hardly for industrially developed—societies; its peculiar merits lie in the blend of traditional Confucianism with a specially tailored version of Marxism, and in its emphasis on agricultural development alongside the growth of an industrial base. Marxism à la Jugoslave has some obvious attractions for western socialists, but does not seem any more able than capitalist or neo-capitalist societies to cope with the general problems of

inflation and resource allocation. None of the other variants of Marxism on offer seems sufficiently relevant or important to warrant special comment. (For some more comment on the Soviet alternative, see the first part of the next chapter.)

8

From Social Contract
to Corporate State

In the last chapter I examined, and rejected, some of the more radical alternatives to the growth-oriented society which exists, in different forms, in the capitalist west and in the Soviet bloc. Moreover, I argued that, with all its weaknesses, the western version of this society offered better prospects than the Communist version. The main reason for the superiority (as I conceive it) of the western model is that it provides for an open, democratic process of decision-making, rather than (as in the Soviet alternative) a closed, authoritarian process. When western systems degenerate into autocracies, they lose this advantage. Therefore, any solution to the problems of post-Keynesian society must, in my judgement, take place within a democratic framework. It is from this standpoint that, in this chapter, I examine various ways in which the ills of this society can be tackled without departing from the fundamental principles on which it is based.

The failures of the socio-economic system in the 1970s originate, if my thesis is right, in its inability to perform up to the expectations of an increasingly impatient and demanding public. If this is so, it would be idle to look for a solution through deliberately reducing the rate of growth through deflationary policies, such as would result from a strict application of Friedmanite monetarist principles—i.e. by reducing the amount of money available for spending, in both the public and the private sector. Such a policy, if carried out in isolation, would reduce both the demand and the supply side of the economic equation. It might therefore achieve an *economic* balance between demand and supply, at a low rate of activity, involving considerable under-use of resources (including manpower). But it would do so at the cost of exacerbating *social* frustration and friction, and the consequences for western society could be lethal. (This is not to say that policies for controlling the money supply have no part to play in a package solution for our problems; as I have already indicated, they can have an essential if secondary role.)

Similarly, my analysis excludes the possibility of solving the present crisis by seeking to move from a growth-oriented to a zero-growth economy, on the grounds that the blow to expectations would not only be deeply damaging to social cohesion, but would almost certainly make such a policy politically non-viable.[1] (Again, this by no means excludes the need to re-orient the *pattern* of growth in western society, in order to direct it towards activities which would play a more helpful role in raising the quality of life and protecting the environment.)

At the same time, we have to reject any purely Keynesian solution to the crisis, in terms of stimulating or depressing the overall level of demand, in order to ensure a better balance of resources. There is indeed no Keynesian solution to the present situation, which combines a high rate of inflation with a high level of unemployment; since the orthodox Keynesian answer to the former would be to reduce demand, and to the latter to increase it. A computer programmed to provide Keynesian answers to today's problems would blow up! (Once again, this is not to say that, in any package solution to the crisis, Keynesian measures of demand regulation would not have a role to play; of course they would, but only once a basic balance had been restored.)

There is another school of economists whose views need to be taken into account. These are the *structuralists*—represented in the UK today by, among others, Robert Bacon and Walter Eltis—who argue that the present imbalance in the western economic system reflects the excessive concentration of resources in the non-market sector dominated by the State; and that a precondition for revival is therefore to reduce public expenditure and employment in the non-market public sector, so that these resources become available once more for wealth creation. There is no doubt, as we have seen already, that the concentration of excessive resources in the State sector has been one of the consequences of the breakdown of the Keynesian system, and that it has to be reversed, even at the cost of some transitional unemployment. But this deals only with one element of the crisis, and in any case, as we have seen, the issue is complicated by the emergence of structural unemployment, which seems to call for a *bigger* State investment.

Lastly, more for the sake of symmetry than of logic, one must mention an alternative economic explanation for the present crisis, which lays the blame at the door of the multinational companies, who have allegedly used their economic power to bid up prices and profits excessively in recent years, and so precipitated inflation. A glance at the trend in profitability of large companies throughout the western world in the past decade, adjusted to allow for inflation, would suggest that if the multinationals have the power ascribed to them, and the single-minded determination to use it to maximise profits to an extreme degree, their managers have displayed an ineptitude in pursuing this objective which borders on the criminal! The multinationals, like other companies, have been among the victims of the crisis, rather than the villains—though they have perhaps been able to protect their position a little better than companies restricted to a single national market.[2]

Restoring the Political Balance

In short, while economic measures must form *part* of any solution to what is basically a crisis of society, they cannot provide the *complete* solution. If we are to move from the economic to the *political* level, there are of course a number of possible solutions to be canvassed. The simplest is to seek to rectify the present imbalance of power between the State and employers on the one hand, and trade unions and other pressure groups on the other, by legislative or authoritarian means. The 'soft' version of such a policy would be to say that the monopoly bargaining power of trade unions creates a fundamental imbalance, which the State is entitled to offset by legislation. Thus the State has the right and duty to impose wage controls, breaches of which could be punished by fining or imprisoning all those party to illegal agreements, or by driving enterprises conceding excessive increases into bankruptcy by preventing them from passing on cost increases to consumers, denying them access to government funds or purchases, and so on; alternatively, the State could announce that a certain amount of money would be available in any one year for wage increases, and if the amount was exceeded the government would simply 'freeze' the increase, by claiming it back in taxes, national insurance contribution surcharges, or similar means. (This would be the monetarists' solution.)

The difficulty about such a policy is to see how, *in the absence of a political consensus*, it could be enforced in a democratic society. One does not correct an imbalance of power simply by ruling it illegal. And so the 'soft' version leads on to the 'hard' version, which is to say that if democracies cannot control inflation they must turn themselves into dictatorships. Trade union power is then limited, not by acts of parliament, but by the secret police and the firing squad.

If inflation proves uncontrollable over a prolonged period of time, the death of democracy becomes quite a likely scenario, for all the reasons discussed in earlier chapters. For most of us, this solution would be worse than the disease; and the survival of democracy in the advanced industrial countries during the current crisis—and the movement away from totalitarianism towards democracy in Greece and Iberia over this period—testifies to the strength of this feeling. But elsewhere, in Latin America and Asia, where democracy has shallower roots and social cohesion is weaker, the trend has been the other way. We should not think it cannot happen here. It could, and it may.

The alternatives to a failed democracy are authoritarianism or anarchy.

But totalitarian regimes themselves have to take account of the deep currents of desire which have generated inflation in the open societies of the west. They are not immune from the fever, as the present troubles of Communist societies show; indeed in some ways they are increasingly vulnerable to it.

There are two reasons for this. First, the growth in consumer living standards has been held back for so long in the Soviet bloc in favour of the public sector, that the pent-up demand is far greater than in the relatively saturated, if still unsatisfied, west. Second, the ability of the productive system to meet these demands is far less. It is less, not just because Soviet-bloc enterprises have less capital installed to meet consumer needs. More important, their managers are ill equipped to respond to consumer demands, because they have never had to operate in a market economy. The planned economy operated by the Soviet bloc can only tolerate a very limited degree of innovation, of individual initiative, of creativity, of market-oriented responses, because such activities disrupt the prearranged pattern of allocation of resources. More-over, there can only be a climate of innovation and creativity where there is a high degree of personal freedom—freedom to travel and absorb new ideas, and a free capital market to back risk ventures.

None of these things can exist, except at the extreme margins, in the Soviet bloc, because the conditions for their existence and toleration would not only imperil the allocative role of the central planners, but would also carry with them the infection of western demands for a better quality of life. So the price for a low overt inflation rate is a resistance to innovation, which is making the Soviet bloc more and more technologically backward *vis-à-vis* the west, and which will increasingly penalise it as it moves away from a manufacturing-dominated economy operating in con-ditions of consumer goods shortage, into a post-manufacturing economy in which basic consumer needs have been met, and the demand is for increasing quality, variety and novelty.

The Soviet system is rather well designed for an agrarian society which wants to establish a primitive manufacturing base very quickly, and is prepared to subordinate other considerations to this end. It is very badly designed for a knowledge-based service economy; and above all, it seems to lack the ability for peaceful evolution, because of the concentration of power in the hands of a single group of managers whose skill lies entirely in the operation of the existing system. Thus the pace of change which a Communist system can manage is extremely slow. The Hungarians have been able to move, if painfully slowly, towards an economic system which does provide some scope for flexibility and market-orientation, though without any vestige of political freedom. The Czechs, trying to move more swiftly in 1968, had to be forcibly suppressed, for fear that their example would infect other parts of the bloc. What all this means is that, when change does come in the Soviet bloc—and come some day it certainly will—the effects will be violent, disruptive, and probably bloody.

Whatever their frustrations, the citizens of the west would be very unwise to despair of democracy and to hanker after totalitarian solutions. Totalitarianism may provide a temporary period of stability for the ruling elites, but at the price almost certainly of a growing technological backwardness, and violent change at some future date. (This is not to say that the French and Italians should never, under any circumstances, entrust their Communist Parties with power. It may be, though one cannot be sure, that these parties are evolving into the kinds of bodies that could exercise power in a democratic framework, without seeking to subvert the institutions which brought them to power.)

Towards a Social Consensus

So I believe we are left with one solution. It is to seek to involve all the major interests and sectors of democratic society in a consensus about the way in which that society should distribute its resources, and the goals which it should seek to follow. If I have correctly interpreted the causes of the present inflationary fever, it springs from the breakdown of an established and recognised social order, in which the distribution of resources enjoyed the sanction of custom and religion, and in which the masses were largely ignorant of the options open to them. The sanctions of religion and custom have gone, so far as one can tell irretrievably, and the former ignorance and limited horizons of the masses have gone too, to be replaced by a greedy hedonism which demands more from the productive system than it can supply. The ensuing conflict over the distribution of the fruits of the productive system poses the biggest threat of internal disruption in western society since the religious wars of the seventeenth century.

We cannot overcome this conflict by narrowing the field of decision-making as in totalitarian systems, but rather by widening it and making it more democratic. We have to confront all our citizens with the real options available, and to try on this basis to establish a realistic consensus. We have to apply the 'stakeholder' concept which we discussed in Chapter 4, in the context of the individual enterprise, to the macro-level of the State. For the automatic consensus of the past, based on religion, custom, inertia and ignorance, we have to substitute a conscious politically-derived consensus, based on free will and informed discussion.

In fact during the last few years every western country has been groping towards this concept. In West Germany it is called the 'social market economy' (*Sozialmarktswirtschaft*). In the UK it is called the 'social contract'. The parties to the social contract (I shall use the phrase during the rest of the book to describe the general process, not the particular British version currently in force) are initially the government and the trade unions, though almost invariably the employer organisations become involved as a third party at some stage. The starting point of the discussion in each case is a joint recognition of the self-defeating nature of inflation, the risks that it involves for all concerned, and the consequent necessity to achieve a solution which will ensure national viability, and at the same time meet as many as possible of the demands of the unions' members.

Because the social and institutional structure is different in each western country, the form and nature of the dialogue show many different national variations. In Japan and France, for example, the trade union movements are relatively weak, and national consensus tends to be reached by a different path—through detailed planning agreements between the government and the large industrial enterprises; though the French government, mindful of 1968 and aware of the growing strength of the political Left, has been trying to broaden the dialogue—and the Seventh French National Plan, published in 1976, establishes a number of very important social objectives for which it seeks a national consensus.

In the US, with its enormous size and diversity, consensus is not something to be formally reached between the Federal government and the leaders of industry and the unions, but rather something which evolves through the political process, to which both sides of industry are expected to contribute. All successful US presidents tend to be consensus presidents, and President Carter is pre-eminently a respecter of this tradition.

In Scandinavia, West Germany, Austria, the Netherlands and the UK, the unions are recognised as being one of the central arbiters of national policy, and social contracts of one form or another constitute a central objective of government—with employers involved in the dialogue, though in a somewhat secondary role. In the Netherlands and Scandinavia social contracts have operated with varying degrees of success, for most of the post-war period. In Italy, because of the weakness of government, the crucial dialogue tends to be between the central leaders of the employer and trade union organisations, who present their agreed conclusions to government almost as a *fait accompli*. This has in the past tended to be the fashion also in Sweden (not in this case out of governmental weakness, but by deliberate choice), but more recently the Swedish government has begun to play a more active role in the dialogue.

It is significant that those countries which have gone furthest down the social contract/consensus road are in most cases those where the trade union movement is most heavily committed to participation in industrial decision-making; indeed, in almost all cases the spread of participation agreements is seen as an aspect of consensus, as part of the social contract.

All social contracts contain an element of wages policy—inevitably, as one of the prime objectives is to prevent wage demands from pushing up national costs to a point at which the national economy ceases to be competitive on world markets. In certain cases, as in the UK in 1975–76, the trade unions have accepted (and enforced on their members) wage increases which were below the rate of price increases, and thus involved a fall in real living standards. But the UK is by no means the leading exponent of income-limiting social contracts. Perhaps the outstanding success story has been West Germany, where the trade unions year after year have agreed to wage increases which are significantly below those of Germany's EEC partners, thereby ensuring German industry a competitive advantage and West Germany a permanent payments surplus.

In return for wage restraint, the trade unions in all the countries operating social contract policies have secured an influential voice in the determination of overall policy objectives. This has included governments' commitment to the various aspects of industrial democracy described in Chapter 4—worker participation at board level and on the shopfloor, the development of a comprehensive framework of labour law, the extension of social protection systems, in some cases support for proposals for compulsory profit-sharing by enterprises. The net effect has been to erode very deeply the traditional management prerogatives within the private sector of the European economy (outside Europe the attack on such prerogatives has been very muted so far), and to substitute power-sharing for managerial autocracy. It remains to be seen what the long-term effects of this rather revolutionary change will be.

Outside the business sector, the trade unions have acquired through the social contract a considerable influence on the broad thrust of government social and economic policy. They can expect to be consulted on the projected rate of economic growth, the priorities to be followed in social expenditure, major changes in the tax system, employment targets and so on.

To say that this influence is entirely a *quid pro quo* for wage restraint is to over-simplify a complex process. It would ignore, for example, the important fact that most of the governments which have successfully pursued social contract policies have been headed by Social Democrats or Socialists, whose party links with the trade unions were in any case strong.

It also ignores the fact that, as mentioned above, employer organisations have also tended to become parties to the social contract. They too have expected to be consulted on overall social and economic policy, though their influence on national decision-making has nowhere been as strong as that of the unions. The employers have of course had to make significant concessions as part of the social contract. Wage restraint has normally been accompanied by some degree of restriction on profits and by some measure of price control. The gains made by the unions in the area of industrial democracy and participation have been at the employers' expense. But governments have found themselves compelled to include employers in the dialogue, if only because economic growth and employment depend crucially on decisions on investment policy made by the boards of enterprises. As we saw in Chapter 4, if governments want growth they have to take account of the views and needs of the business sector, since it is only this sector which has the means to generate growth. So government has to try to see that business has the resources and the confidence to create growth, and this must condition the measures adopted to restrain prices and profits. Such measures have to be strong enough to satisfy the unions that their restraint is not unilateral, yet moderate enough to assure industry of the resources needed to finance re-investment and expansion. It is not an easy balance to strike.

So, if the social contract is a bargain, it is a bargain of a very complex kind. Yet, in its essence, it is indeed a bargain, in which the unions trade income restraint for an increase in power and influence throughout the economy and social system, gains achieved partly at the expense of employers and partly at the expense of the sovereignty of parliament (which means in effect the autonomy of government). The bargain the trade unions would *like* to strike is one which trades restraint for a guarantee of jobs. But in the present climate of high—and, in some countries, still rising—unemployment, that is a bargain no government would be able to honour. To put it more precisely, in present circumstances it seems impossible to establish a wage rate which will (a) significantly reduce unemployment, and (b) prove politically acceptable at a time of steeply rising prices.

Nevertheless, during the dark days of high inflation and high unemployment, when government is reducing public spending in order to free resources for future growth, and in order to reduce its money requirements, an exception is likely to be made for measures to stimulate jobs, even if only of a token nature. And, as and when the social contract and associated measures start to bear fruit and inflation rates come down, the probability is that future social contracts will focus increasingly on the link between income restraint and job creation.

It seems to me clear that the stresses which have come near to destroying the Keynesian system can only be effectively cured by some form of social contract, to restore the balance of power in society, to re-establish a social consensus and secure agreement on the broad policy objectives to be followed. However, the approach is not without its own dangers for the future of society, and these should be examined before we proceed further blithely down this road.

Critics of the Social Contract

The arguments against the social contract approach are of varying kinds, and some of them are mutually contradictory.

Thus one school of thought argues that the nature of our society prevents either trade union or employer central organisations exercising the kind of authority over their members which the social contract requires. Thus, it is argued, the central organisations are like a stage army, carrying out a charade of negotiations with the government, while in fact they totally lack the authority which they pretend to have. The Confederation of British Industry (CBI) may argue with the government about conditions which would justify investment by its members, but the actual investment decisions are taken by boards of directors without any reference to the CBI. Similarly, the TUC may undertake on behalf of its members to exercise wage restraint, but it has no power to prevent individual unions or small groups of workers from securing wage increases which are quite incompatible with the contract.

There is of course an element of truth in this argument, and it would be a sad day for the economy and our society if the degree of local autonomy which exists were to be steam-rollered out of existence by central juggernauts. But in fact the events of recent years have shown that the central organisations on both sides do have considerable moral authority over their members, provided that commitments are submitted to a detailed process of internal debate and reflect a consensus within the organisation. Thus the CBI *did* operate unilaterally a voluntary price control policy between 1971 and 1972, in conditions of accelerating world inflation, in return for government measures to reflate the economy. In 1975 and 1976 the TUC *did* operate a voluntary policy of wage restraint which was honoured virtually without exception by its member unions, even if they had opposed the policy, during a period when real living standards were falling. And on the Continent, in Germany and the Scandinavian countries for example, income restraint policies have been enforced by trade unions without any legislative sanction, with a very high degree of internal discipline.

In assessing the effectiveness of the 'social partners'—as the employer and union organisations are called in contemporary Continental jargon—as political agents, there would seem to be four determining factors. These are:

(1) The degree of institutional centralisation. In the Scandinavian countries and West Germany there are a relatively small number of trade unions, tidily organised in different, noncompeting sectors of the economy. In such circumstances, internal coherence and discipline are much easier to achieve than in the British union movement, with several hundred trade unions, many of them coexisting in single industries, sometimes in active competition for membership.

(2) The nature of the commitment required. Trade unions can on occasions make and keep firm commitments on wages, and employer organisations (though less easily) on prices. But there is very little a central employers' organisation can do to influence the investment decisions of its members; and the influence of central trade unions on the performance of their members on the shop-floor, the readiness or otherwise to operate effective productivity agreements, and so on, is likewise limited. If government wishes to exercise a decisive influence in these areas, over and above the indirect influence of national policy measures, it must find ways of bypassing the central social partner organisations, and talk directly to the decision-makers—directors and shop stewards—at the level of the individual enterprise.

(3) The environment in which decisions are taken. Social partners are more ready to take on, and honour, commitments if they are convinced (a) that they will get something in return, (b) that the situation is serious enough to warrant a special effort. Thus social contract policies are easier to introduce in times of crisis than in times of relaxation. Since the central social partner organisations are representative bodies, time has to be allowed for an internal consensus to be agreed, if it is to be effective. Once it is operational a social contract policy will succeed only to the extent that it is seen to be producing the results which the parties expected. Thus, where such policies are seen to benefit both the economy as a whole and the main individual groups within it—as has tended to be the case in West Germany and Scandinavia—the habit of consensus grows and begins to be absorbed into the national cultural bloodstream; civilising, as in Scandinavia, all the confrontation aspects of society (witness the low strike rate and high degree of industrial relations harmony in countries like Sweden and West Germany). But where consensus policies lead to what is interpreted as undue sacrifice by one or other section—either because the agreement was badly drawn up initially, or because exogenous factors intervene (imported inflation or depression, for example)—they will tend to go sour, and to leave a legacy of mutual mistrust which makes their future resuscitation

more difficult. There is nothing very surprising in this. No voluntary agreement can survive too much strain or distortion. Success breeds success, failure breeds failure. There is no magic in social contract policies. They are, after all, the product of fallible human beings.

(4) The degree of pre-existing social harmony. Any bargain is easier to strike, and to maintain, if the bargainers share certain common assumptions and attitudes, and if there is a certain element of trust between them. Social contracts are no exception. It is no accident that the societies which have found it easiest to follow consensus policies are those where class divisions are least pronounced, where governments tend to be social democratic in tone, where the leaders of trade unions and employers come from a class and educational background not too dissimilar. We have already noted the rather close relationship between policies of national consensus and industrial participation. The two tend to go together, and to grow fastest in societies which enjoy a certain degree of social equality, without the harsh class stratifications which exist, for example, in Italy or France, and in a more limited degree in the UK. In this latter group of countries, workers' loyalties tend to focus on their class leaders and comrades, and they find it much harder to identify with the boss, or with the community as a whole. In such societies it is natural for trade unions to adopt a conflictive rather than a consensus role, and it is in such societies that Marxism finds its most fertile ground.

If, in societies of this latter group, the leaders of the trade unions find themselves in a situation where it is in their interest to negotiate a social contract, they will find it harder than in less class-conscious societies to carry their members with them, and harder therefore to carry conviction as partners in government. In such societies consensus may indeed be reached at the top, but it risks remaining a consensus of elites, not fully reflected down the line, and therefore highly fragile. The union leaders have to beware of getting too remote from their members, and they have to spend proportionally more time and effort in internal communication, if the social contract is to hold.

This is indeed the situation which exists today in Italy,[3] and to some extent in the UK—though in the British case there are many ambiguities in the situation. Britain has always been a country of sharp class differences—no doubt in part because the middle classes tend to educate their children in different schools from the masses, so that class divisions become evident very early in a child's life. These differences in attitude and culture persist despite a rather high degree of equality in earnings after tax. At the same time the *political*, as opposed to the *social*, climate favours consensus, since the Labour Party which has dominated the British political scene for most of the time since 1964 is closely linked with the TUC, as is the case in Germany and Scandinavia. Thus the British political landscape resembles that of the Nordic countries, but the social landscape is more reminiscent of the Latins. It is this ambiguity in the British situation which renders the issue of consensus versus confrontation policies such an intricate and controversial one in our country today.

The question of the effectiveness of the social partners can therefore only be answered in a conditional way. *If* all the conditions are right, experience seems to suggest, they can be effective participants in the process of government. But if the necessary conditions are not met, they will be ineffective, and in these circumstances a social contract is bound to become a form of window-dressing, an evasion of reality, and as such, counter-productive.

Broadening the Consensus

In any case (and here we come to the second argument against the social contract as currently envisaged), why should the big producers' organisations—the employers and the trade unions—have an exclusive right to make policy in the social and economic field with the government? What about the many whose interests are unrepresented by these groups—the retired, the self-employed, consumers, non-unionised workers, small firms, and so on? By what right are these groups excluded from the magic circle? And would the dialogue not in any case be enriched if their voices could be heard?

The first answer to this must be that there is no reason in equity or logic why the social contract should be limited—just as there is no reason why the issue of boardroom representation at the level of the enterprise should be confined to the single aspect of worker participation. It is to be hoped that as the habit of consensus policy-making develops, more and more 'social partners' can be identified and brought into the policy-making circuit. But one has to start somewhere—and it so happens that the employer and worker interests are the most important economically, and the best organised, in most industrial societies today.[4]

There are two variants of the argument against social partner exclusivity that are, however, particularly important. The first concerns the threat, real or apparent, which the 'Corporate State' (the State in which the key decisions are taken by the representatives of the great producer interests in conjunction with government) presents to parliamentary democracy.

The dilemma is a real one. On the one hand, the leaders of the TUC and CBI, and their equivalents in other countries, embody, as we have seen, real if limited power. If government is going to manage the economy effectively, it needs their agreement, and it has to be prepared to pay a price to get it. On the other hand, these gentlemen have no brief to represent that large part of the population who are outside their organisations, and they have in no sense been elected to represent the nation. If government, in order to govern effectively, is going to frame policy in conjunction with them, it is bound in certain areas to bypass parliament, which is supposed to represent the will of the nation, and to give to non-elected representatives of special interest groups an authority denied to the elected representatives of the whole people.

One can argue against this that parliament retains the ultimate authority to dismiss the government, which it is the more likely to exercise the more the government is seen to be ignoring it. Legislation has to be approved by parliament, and outside the areas covered by the social contract the rights and authority of parliament are totally unimpaired. The delegation of power from parliament is real, but limited; and there are many institutional ways in which parliament can be associated more closely with the process of economic consensus—for example, by a more liberal use of parliamentary committees. The Corporate State and parliamentary democracy are by no means irreconcilable.

At the same time, it *is* true that the authority of parliament has declined, with the growth of the great producer interest groups or 'social partners'. This is partly because of the special links which trade unions tend to have with socialist or social democratic parties, and the fact that these parties have tended to form the government for most of the time in most European countries since the mid-1960s. But it is also because of the vital importance in the economic area of consistency and continuity in government policy. It is this above all which industrialists in all countries seek from government, as a condition for undertaking investment and risk-ventures. Guarantees of policy continuity are hard to reconcile with the adversary tradition which conditions party politics as reflected in parliament—particularly in countries like Britain, where the political debate is polarised between two major parties, each of which expects to form the government for significant periods.

It is much easier to establish consensus, and a basis of policy continuity against which business can plan, when the political options are limited. This is the case, either when a single party has an exceptionally long period in power—as in post-war Japan, or France since the Fifth Republic was established in 1957, or in Sweden during the forty-year rule of the Social Democrats which ended in 1976—or when the balance of power is such as to make coalition government inevitable (as tends to be the case in countries with proportional representation systems). Coalition governments are the norm in West Germany, Austria and the Benelux countries, and as a result there is a high degree of political stability and continuity. In West Germany, for example, the party which has had the longest period in office since 1945 has been neither of the two giant parties, the Christian Democrats or the Social Democrats; but the relatively small centre party, the Free Democrats, who have served as junior coalition partners with both the CDU and the SPD in turn, and have prevented both of them in turn from moving too far away from centrist policies. (By contrast, the British equivalent of the FPD, the Liberal Party, though it attracts a rather bigger share of the total vote in general elections, has never been in office since 1945, and does not look at all likely to be so.)[5] Thus the British two-party system encourages sharp fluctuations in policy, while the proportional representation system practised in many Continental countries encourages continuity. The latter is a much more fertile ground for nurturing social and economic consensus.

At the same time, whatever its failings parliament does represent the interests of the people as a whole, and this is a right which must not be abrogated in the interests of a consensus of producer groups—however much the antics of the party machines may seem to have distorted and prostituted it, and weakened the credibility of parliament as the forum of public debate. Mrs Thatcher, the Leader of the British Conservative Party, is right when she insists that in a parliamentary democracy institutions as such have no rights; only people can have rights. So the social partners, in their incarnation as agents of the Corporate State, have to be restrained by an alert and vigorous parliament. But it is for parliament to ensure that it is capable of exercising this role, by modifying its procedures and, where necessary, loosening the bonds of party discipline.

The Risk of Immobilisme

This is the more necessary because of the evident danger that the Corporate State can ossify into a condition of *immobilisme*, a frozen posture in which the conflicting interests of the big pressure groups can only be accommodated by accepting a state of paralysis, a perpetuation of the *status quo*, since any change will upset the balance to the disadvantage of one or other of the dinosaurs. This is a real danger for the Corporate State, and it represents the most serious of the arguments against it.

I have referred already, in the previous chapter, to the dangers of 'institutional lag'—the tendency of all human institutions, especially representative ones, to give a greater weight to stability than to change, and to respond too slowly to the external pressures—and opportunities—of a rapidly changing environment. The 'social partners' are in no way immune from this danger—in fact, in many ways they are highly vulnerable to it. Trade unions are by their nature conservative bodies. Employers' associations are bound to give a special weight to those of their members who feel threatened by change, as opposed to the more aggressive ones who stand to gain from it—if only because it is the former who will tend to lobby them most strongly. The aggressive tend to be individualists, the 'clubbable' and collectivists to be the more conservative. Thus it is not surprising that trade associations and employer groups tend to reflect the lowest common denominator among their members.

The more powerful these groups become, therefore, the greater the danger that the dynamic element in the community, the innovators, will find more obstacles placed in their path. It need not be so. The events of the last few years show that, in appropriate conditions, both unions and employer organisations can be weaned away from defensive postures if they are faced with clear alternatives by government. But the danger is always there, and it has to be said that if the price of consensus is frustration of innovation and dynamism, it is too expensive.

Let me be more specific. In an inflationary situation, one of the main benefits from a social contract will be an agreed policy of income and price restraint. Such a policy has to be policed. It must be relatively simple. It cannot afford to be too flexible, to contain too many exceptions. Yet if it is too inflexible, it can destroy the ability of the economy to respond to outside forces, by atrophying the mechanism by which resources move to where they can be most productive.

We have already seen, in Chapter 4, how the role of the price mechanism and of profits has been distorted by the efforts of governments to restrain inflation by controlling prices and profits. The harm which this can do, if continued too rigidly over too long a period, is manifest. Not only can profit restriction destroy incentive and motivation. Relative prices are the signalling system in a market economy which brings demand and supply into alignment, and influences resource allocation in the most effective and flexible way. If this signalling system is put out of commission, the economy loses the ability to react, and to order its forces in the optimum way. It becomes fossilised.

The same applies in the case of incomes (of which, of course, profits form a part). Wages and salaries are the price of labour, and like other prices they are the means by which labour is allocated to those sectors of the economy where it can be most productive—as well as being a reward for effort, and an incentive. If the economy is not to atrophy, therefore, systems of income determination (including the tax system) must retain enough flexibility to enable the labour market to operate as a resource allocator and a skill promoter.

Any incomes policy must embody the attributes of *fairness* and *flexibility*. The concept of 'fairness', or social justice, is very basic in human preoccupations—perhaps even more basic than the concept of liberty—and it is the moral basis for all social contract policies. A social contract which is thought to be 'unfair' cannot survive in a democracy. But what is 'fairness' in this context? It implies, first of all, an element of *discipline* or control. If I am to accept certain limitations on my freedom, I must be assured that others are accepting the same restraints. Thus, an incomes policy has to be controlled if it is to be effective, and the stricter the control the less scope for flexibility and exceptions.

Beyond this, 'fairness' implies two concepts which are at least to some extent mutually contradictory. On the one hand, for most people the fairest way to share things out is to distribute them equally. Thus any voluntary incomes policy is likely to have a strong egalitarian element in it, since the most obviously morally defensible distribution system is one based on the principle of equality. At the same time, there is a general underlying belief that people should be rewarded for special effort or special circumstances, and this belief is often expressed in a very conservative way. If a person or a group of people have enjoyed special differentials in the past, there is a strong public presumption that they should continue doing so. Thus it is possible to build into an incomes policy special differentials for two reasons—as an incentive for special effort or achievement, or to attract people to special jobs; or as a recognition that such differentials have traditionally been enjoyed, and people enjoying them therefore have legitimate expectations that they should be preserved. But there is obviously a limit beyond which one cannot run the principle of differentials in harness with that of equality; and, because we are dealing here with attitudes which are not precisely formulated, and which are subject to influences from the mass media and other areas, it is very hard to apply the principles in a way which can be assured of popular support.

In other words, the construction of an incomes policy which responds both to social criteria and economic needs is an inherently difficult task. What makes it harder is that the labour market is an international one, but one where the degree of international mobility is greater for some types of workers than for others. Those with the highest degree of mobility tend to be those with special skills—managers or professionally qualified people. Thus the market rate for these people tends to be set by international standards, which may be quite out of line with the rates corresponding to the incomes policies in force in particular countries. The UK in 1976 constitutes a good example of this situation. The relatively low growth of the British economy, and a highly egalitarian tax structure and incomes policy, have depressed take-home pay for managers and professionally qualified people to a level well below the world market rate. Thus the dilemma facing the framers of the UK social contract is plain. Either the contract is modified to make a special exception for this group—which is already of course near the top of the UK income scale—in recognition of the opportunities open to it elsewhere; or we risk a major loss of talent to overseas jobs via a 'brain drain'. To take the first course would offend against the principle of fairness, as seen by most British trade unionists; to take the second course would be economically—and in the long term, socially also—highly disadvantageous.

So the maintenance of an effective incomes policy is beset with problems. The concepts on which it is based are to a considerable extent mutually contradictory, and compromises have to be struck between them. Exceptions to the basic principles may have to be made, because of the bargaining strengths of particular groups (miners, power station engineers?), or because of the need to match competing salaries abroad (doctors, managers?), or for other reasons. But how many exceptions can be made without discrediting the policy? How can one reconcile the instinct to-wards fairness and equality with the need to provide flexibility, to reward initiative, skill and effort, and to create incentives for innovation and risk-taking? How can one combine social justice with the requirements of a dynamic society?[6]

There is no cut-and-dried formula which can answer these questions. A social contract is not a panacea for the problems of post-Keynesian society. It may well be a *necessary* condition for the solution of many of these problems; I believe it is. But it is certainly not a *sufficient* condition, and if the necessary precautions are not taken it could produce a cure worse than the disease. We have to ensure at all costs that consensus policies do not lead to *immobilisme*, that the social contract does not generate the abuses of the Corporate State, freezing the economy into an over-centralised, undemocratic straitjacket, and creating unscaleable barriers to change and innovation.

This is the challenge. How are we to meet it?

NOTES TO CHAPTER 8

[1] But see note 2 to Chapter 7.

[2] Of course it is true that, in so far as there has been a process of concentration among fewer producers in certain important product and factor markets, so that there are fewer direct competitors in key sectors, firms have been able to push up prices faster than they could otherwise have done—and this may have made them less willing to resist cost increases which they knew they could, if

necessary, pass on to the consumer. Increased international competition has led, in some cases, to increased monopoly, as weaker firms have been forced out of production. 'Competition', as the nineteenth-century French economist Proudhon argued, 'kills competition'. At the same time there has been greater invasion of some product markets by others—plastics invading markets formerly reserved for natural textiles or metals, for example—so that the picture is by no means a simple one. However, it is undoubtedly true that, over the western world as a whole, the sector of the economy where prices are determined by producers' decisions—the area described by J. K. Galbraith in *The New Industrial State* as the 'technostructure', where prices are 'administered' —is growing at the expense of what Galbraith calls the 'market sector', where there are so many small competitors that no one of them can individually determine prices. Where prices are normally 'administered', there is of course a stronger *prima facie* case for governmental intervention in price determination than there is in the 'market' sector, where prices depend on the demand-and-supply relationship of the market.

3 A special feature of the Italian situation is the distrust which Italian unions and employers have of legislation, and the relative lack of interest therefore in the extension of labour law or of legally-enforced worker participation in management. The reason is that in Italy there is a long, and not entirely dishonourable, tradition of non-observance of the law. I say 'not entirely dishonourable', because for much of its history the administration of justice in large parts of Italy has been corrupt, alien and oppressive; and even today the system is creaky and inefficient.

4 It is also true that the smaller units in society—the small firms and self-employed—which normally live within Galbraith's 'market' sector of the economy, cannot contribute directly to cost-push inflation on an important scale. They are therefore normally immune from the institutional restraints on wage and price inflation imposed by governments, and to that extent they become, as it were, spectators of and reactors to, rather than participants in, the dramas of the social contract and the Corporate State. The discussion in this chapter refers essentially to Galbraith's 'technostructure'. We should not forget the existence alongside it of the 'market sector' of small units, whose survival and prosperity still depends, as it always did, on the forces of competition.

5 The electoral pact established between the Labour Government and the Liberal Party in 1977, for tactical reasons, has given the UK for the first time since 1945 an approximation to the German situation.

6 In fact I suspect part of the answer lies in the interaction between the 'techno-structure' and the 'market' systems. In other words, as the larger units in our

economies become more unionised, more politicised, less able to adjust their labour forces to respond to market changes, we will see growing up alongside them much smaller, specialised, entrepreneurial enterprises, living in highly competitive conditions, probably non-unionised—like pilot-fish in symbiotic relationships with leviathan. More and more, I suspect, it will suit the large companies to sub-contract work to these 'pilot-fish' operators, especially if the alternative is to take on more labour on what might prove to be a temporary basis. It is from this entrepreneurial sector that much of the dynamism in the economy of the 1980s may come.

9
The Rational Society

The troubles which have befallen western society in the past decade are essentially due to the breakdown of disciplines which previously protected the economic order. The Keynesian system after 1945 replaced the automatic disciplines of the classical economic system with a hierarchy of man-made disciplines; during the past decade these have come increasingly under challenge, to a point at which the survival of civilisation as we know it is under threat. The first social priority, therefore, must be the restoration of economic order, based on a generally acceptable structure of disciplines (including, crucially, monetary discipline). This structure has to be created by agreement between the various groups which make up society, notably—but not exclusively—the major producer interests. This agreement I call, without originality, the *social contract*.

Any social contract has to respond to the pressures felt in society. It must, therefore, in my view give a high priority to achieving a satisfactory rate of economic growth, since only by this means can the demands of society (including the demand for more jobs) begin to be met. For this reason we must reject the siren calls of the 'zero-growth' school. The contract must ensure, on the economic side, that adequate resources are devoted to capital investment in the wealth-creating sector, as well as to exports and overseas aid. It must enforce a proper control of the money supply. It must, however, also ensure that the growth pattern responds, more than in the past, to social priorities. In other words, growth must not be pursued at the expense of environmental pollution, the wasteful use of scarce resources, and so on. The 'external' costs of growth, where they can be identified, must be charged to the perpetrators; and incentives must be provided to entrepreneurs whose activities will lead to social benefits over and above the immediate market return.

We saw in the last chapter some of the risks inherent in the pursuit of social contract policies—that they might work against democracy, against the excluded interests, against the forces of change and innovation which might threaten established producer interests. These are real dangers. The establishment of a legally-protected 'closed shop' system in industry, whereby all employees have to be members of trade unions, may be defended as part of a comprehensive social contract. But in this case are there not issues of individual freedom to be weighed in the scales against those of trade union convenience? Similarly, a social contract might well be used to justify the maintenance of an industrial restrictive price agreement or monopoly, on the grounds that it was needed to preserve jobs and was a part of the nation's industrial structure. But in the long term such forms of protection can help to destroy the creative forces of competition and innovation.

The way to avoid these and other dangers is to ensure that the circle of interests included in the social contract is as broad as possible. The more limited the number of bargainers, the more likely it is that the bargains eventually struck will be restrictive and defensive. The second point is to try to limit the operation of the contract to those matters which are relevant to economic and social performance, and not to bring in extraneous issues which happen to suit the interest of one or other bargainer. The third is to try to involve parliament in the ratification of the contract, and in the continuous review of its operation.

The precise formulae adopted are much less important than the spirit in which society takes its collective decisions on how it wants to allocate its resources, and what priorities it is going to follow. This after all is what this whole book is about. We can no longer leave such decisions to be taken by the impersonal forces of the market, or by governments acting in isolation from the other forces of society, or to the conflicting self-interests of sectional pressure groups. Because power is no longer centralised in our society, and because the decisions and actions of each sector impinge on others, we have to find a way of taking decisions which reflects the long-term interests of society as a whole, as well as the immediate needs of the individual sectors. Ideally such a process should emerge in a democracy from the political dialogue, but for various reasons—the perennial conflict between government and opposition, the power of the party machines, the separation of political power from industrial power—the political system does not reflect the various forces which have to be accommodated if society is to prosper. The political dialogue cannot be replaced, but it needs to be supplemented.

The society which reaches its collective decisions in the manner advocated in this book I call the Rational Society. It seeks to replace the conflict of competing groups by a consensus based on rational discussion and debate. Such a society is only likely to be operable if it already possesses a certain degree of social cohesion. Indeed, it is no accident that the countries which have best survived the great inflation of the last decade, and the ensuing recession, are those which possess a high degree of such cohesion, and which approach nearest to the ideal of the rational society.

Routes to Social Survival

We live in the twilight of dying ideologies. The Christian capitalist ideology of the west and the Marxist ideology of eastern Europe both seem to have lost the dynamic they once had. Strange sparks jump about in the embers, bearing names like Trotskyism, Maoism, revolutionary anarchism, and various brands of nationalism. But the great flames which gave purpose and strength to whole nations have died down, and the ashes are starting to grow cold. Only in eastern Asia, as we have already noted, can we find societies with a genuine sense of purpose, societies which seem to retain an inner dynamic which we have lost. Some of these societies are ostensibly Marxist, some ostensibly capitalist. Their common feature is that their method of decision-taking is collectivist, and that they operate according to an agreed central plan or strategy.

If the societies of the west could find ways of combining this social cohesion with the individualism which lies at the heart of the Christian and capitalist traditions, and which has in the past ensured a high rate of innovation and dynamic change, we could perhaps survive the death of ideology and the vacuum of religious faith—as the Roman empire managed for many centuries to do. That should be the aim of the rational society.

The stakes are very high. If inflation starts to rise again with the revival of trade, if unemployment remains at present levels for a few more years, democracy could become unworkable, to be replaced either by totalitarianism or by Mafia-style anarchy. We have perhaps only a few years to ensure the survival of democracy as we know it.

We are handicapped in our approach to these agonisingly complex problems by the absence of a social dimension to our traditional economic thinking. The economic decisions taken by the Chinese and the Japanese, in their very different ways, reflect agreed social values and criteria. That has not been the approach either of western capitalism, with its profit-maximising objective, or of European Marxism, with its ideal of maximising economic growth and establishing self-sufficient industrial systems. Yet we have seen, throughout this book, that in today's world social and economic factors are inextricably interlinked, and that it is the social which tends to determine the economic rather than vice versa. The reason why Keynesian economic disciplines broke down was that they became socially unacceptable. Once it has been generally accepted that man can control his economic environment, it follows inevitably that economic systems become subservient to social objectives and criteria; and from that point on it is the social system which defines the parameters within which economic decisions can be taken.

At the same time, economic factors determine the progress which can be made towards social objectives. If pursuit of these objectives puts a greater strain on the economic system than it can bear, society is in great trouble.

It must follow, therefore, that economists and social scientists should be working together on the solution of our national problems, and that there should be the maximum cross-fertilisation between the two disciplines. I may be wrong, but I do not detect this happening to any great extent today in western Europe. Economics is the oldest of the social sciences, the one with the longest tradition of access to the centres of power, and with the most impressive body of literature to date. It is not surprising, therefore, that economists tend to be somewhat disdainful of their colleagues in other social disciplines. Moreover, many economists have succumbed to the fatal lure of mathematics, and have pursued abstract quantification at the expense of immersion in the real world of uncertainty, political pressures and irrationality. The lure of the abstract is as old as Plato in western thought. But the concern of the economist, as of other social scientists, should not be with abstract truth. His place is with his fellow-men in Plato's cave, interpreting the shadows thrown on the walls by the ideal world of thought, and trying to organise the furniture and the food supplies to the best advantage of his fellow-sojourners.

The isolation, and the dominance, of economics among the social sciences is evidenced by the very considerable investment by western governments since the war in economic planning. Such plans have been almost entirely devoid of social content, and not surprisingly their record over the last decade has been somewhat dismal. Given the relative importance of the social compared to the economic dimension, and given the mess which, as we have seen, pervades virtually all western social policies at the present time, one would think that at least a fraction of the resources hitherto devoted to economic planning might with advantage be devoted to *social* planning.

We have seen that the investment by governments in social welfare has been producing a less and less satisfactory return; that such investment has been undertaken with only the sketchiest analysis of objectives and alternatives; that the indiscriminate expansion of the welfare state is no longer feasible, and that there has to be in future a much more selective use of funds; and that the social problems in modern society are mounting, with consequent loss of morale and alienation. Surely this situation calls for urgent planning, and for the establishment as quickly as possible of an informed consensus on what needs to be done in the social area. It is hard to envisage a viable long-term social contract which does not concern itself with the priorities in this field; for unless we can tackle social problems more effectively in the next decade than we have in the last, the social cohesion which we need to guide our economic systems may still elude us.

Forms of Social Contract

It is not my purpose in this book to propose blueprints or formulae for the ideal social contract. To do so would make a mockery of my contention that the contract must arise naturally from a social consensus—that it must reflect the wishes of the majority in each country. Not only will each country arrive naturally at a differentiated set of priorities reflecting national means, conditions and aspirations, but the institutional structures appropriate to each country will also differ, depending on history and the political and industrial system. A huge, federal country like the USA, where the trade unions represent a less prominent element in society, will establish its consensus through different channels from the smaller, more centralised, more unionised communities of western Europe.

One can, however, establish certain minimum conditions which are likely to have to be met if consensus is to work. First, any social contract formula has to be seen to be equitable and at the same time flexible; second, it must be seen to be arising from a widely-based dialogue, and not imposed on the rest of the community by a small inner circle of oligarchies; third, it must carry the commitment of the major political parties, so that its survival will not be dependent on—though it must of course reflect—changes in the balance of political power.

In the UK the obvious forum for developing the concept of the social dialogue would be an expanded version of the tripartite National Economic Development Council ('Neddy' in popular parlance), which for the past sixteen years has been responsible for national economic planning, and which is currently (in 1977) working out a national economic strategy.[1] The Council's members include members of the government, TUC, CBI, and some independents (including from time to time a representative of consumer interests).[2] If, as this book argues, economic planning cannot succeed in present conditions without an underpinning of social consensus, the 'Neddy' framework should perhaps be expanded to enable It to embrace a social as well as an economic strategy capability. It is noteworthy that the Seventh French National Plan, covering the period 1976–80, includes, unlike all its predecessors since the war, a section on social objectives and strategy. In other European countries with a tradition of post-war planning, such as the Netherlands, Austria and the Scandinavian countries, the link between social and economic objectives has been clearly seen—as it has in West Germany, despite the ideological inhibition which forbids the government there to admit that it is engaging in national planning while encouraging it to do so in practice (through the use of circumlocutions like 'Concerted Action', 'Medium-Term Programming', etc.).

Each country must find its own institutional solution. Equally, each must find its own formula for the distribution of national income, for the balance of institutional power, for the relationship between the needs of economic freedom and social discipline. In the last chapter I discussed some of the underlying conflicts within wage policy determination—the issue of differentials versus egalitarianism, the role of wage relativities in allocating the labour force, and so on. The correct balance in these matters will alter from time to time, and no formula will be ideal for all time. Economic distortions in the cause of social equity can be borne for short periods, but not indefinitely; the same applies inversely. It is for society to determine the least-bad balance at any one time.

There are various ways by which flexibility can be introduced even into a rigid overall system. For example, one can envisage a system which allows each enterprise to increase its total wage bill by a fixed percentage, but leaves the distribution for the enterprise itself to determine (presumably in consultation with its employees). One could have an ostensibly free system of collective bargaining, while stipulating that any money paid out above an established ceiling would be recouped by the government in taxation: either on the employer (in which case he would have to pay the extra tax by increasing productivity or restricting the wage bill), or on the employee (in which case the money could be 'frozen' like post-war credits in the UK). Each of these formulae has disadvantages. None offers a panacea. The best solution can only be found by a process of trial and error, based on the widest possible public debate.

The Maze and the Minotaur

It is fatally easy, in any discussion of this kind, to get bogged down in the technical intricacies of various forms of incomes policies. The details are of course important, but they are not the essence of the matter. What we are really talking about, in my view, is whether our society has the will to survive. If the will is there, the means can be found.

I am conscious that I have provided no answer in this book to the problems that beset us. What I have tried to do is to analyse the problems that have brought us to this pass, and to suggest, tentatively, ways in which we might start to seek a way out. When Theseus entered the maze in Crete, Ariadne gave him a thread to guide him out. But first he had to kill the Minotaur— and that he had to do on his own. My purpose in this book has been to play Ariadne's role. But the killing of the Minotaur requires virtues beyond the professional ken of economists, social scientists, or students of political institutions. We need courage, patience, a concern and sympathy for our fellow-men, and for the values inherent in our civilisation. We need hope, faith, and more than a little charity.

We are at the end of a historical epoch, and at the dawn of another for which we have as yet no name. We have passed a point of no return. We can move forward to what I have called the Rational Society, but which could equally be called a responsible, mature or a caring society; a society in which there will be more joy and creativity, a better harnessing of the wonders of technology for human happiness.

Or we can move into the dark shadows of paternalism and autocracy, the individual withdrawing from social contact and responsibility into a private fantasy existence (as we see happening all too frequently today in our over-specialised world, not least in our so-called centres of learning). We can insist on our rights under the Welfare State, ignoring our duties and responsibilities— in which case the Welfare State will collapse, as it already threatens to do, under the weight of its unbudgeted commitments.

If our present system is failing, if we are living today through a period of social shock, it is because our present elites—both in western and Communist societies—have failed to understand and cope with the consequences of past technology on present society. That is why today, for example, more than sixty nations are alleged to use torture systematically as a political instrument, why the population of Calcutta is projected to rise to seventy million people when it cannot provide a tolerable livelihood for one-tenth that number, and why in the decade of the Vietnam war twice as many Americans died violent deaths in the US as on the battlefield.[3] We cannot find a solution by slavish conformity to the whims of Big Daddy, or by withdrawing from our social responsibilities, or by seeking scapegoats for the failures of our society among nonconformists or minority groups. We have to build on the democratic shoots of vitality, which spring up perennially in human society, never perhaps more excitingly than today. We have to found our new society on a community of socially mature, responsible individuals, unshackled by the preconceptions of the past. We have to ensure that all our managers, in whatever sector of society, are socially as well as technically trained and aware. We have to build into our social systems techniques of social prevention based on advance warning, instead of relying solely on systems of cure. It is for this that we need a structure of social planning—not to impose on our citizens any particular social pattern.

Shock can be liberating as well as destructive. Perhaps the

traumas through which we are now going will enable us to see clearly that the Minotaur is not a monster external to us, but more a creature of our will, whom our will can destroy if we wish. Have we the imagination, the courage, the generosity to kill the Minotaur, and follow Ariadne's thread to the blue seas and the green meadows beyond?

From what I know of humanity, it doesn't seem impossible.

NOTES TO CHAPTER 9

[1] For economic planning in the UK and the role of NEDC past, present and future, see my *Planning and Politics: The British Experience 1960-1976* (Allen & Unwin 1977).

[2] Since writing these words, I have been appointed to fill this seat on the NEDC.

[3] A recent survey by a team from the Massachusetts Institute of Technology states that one of every eleven children born in the city of Atlanta, Georgia will be murdered if he or she stays there. Murder is now the leading cause of death for young black men in urban areas of the US. On present trends, one of every six males born in Harlem, New York City will be murdered by the age of sixty-five. A male child born in the US is more likely to die by murder than was an American soldier in World War Two to die in combat. Nearly one in five black women can expect to be raped during their lifetime. A single police precinct of New York, with a population of 50,000, has nearly as many murders in a year as the whole of London. Between 1960 and 1975 the overall crime rate in the US for the seven 'index crimes'—murder, rape, robbery, aggravated assault, burglary, larceny and motor vehicle theft—rose by 180%. The number of women arrested for robbery rose by 647% in the same period. Recent polls indicate that crime is the social issue of most concern to Americans. Here we see, in a country of great wealth, economic strength and social-political stability, the sinister advance of the Mafia State.

Bibliography

Bacon, Robert & Eltis, Walter *Britain's Economic Problem* (Macmillan)
Baldelli, Giovanni *Social Anarchism* (Penguin)
Bannock, Graham *The Juggernauts* (Penguin), *How To Survive The Slump* (Penguin)
Beckerman, Wilfred *In Defence of Economic Growth* (Cape)
Bell, Daniel *The Coming of Post-Industrial Society* (Penguin)
Bookchin, Murray *Post-Scarcity Anarchism* (Ramparts)
Chorafas, D. N. *The Knowledge Revolution* (Allen & Unwin)
Clegg, Hugh *How To Run an Incomes Policy* (Penguin)
Craven, Edward (editor) *Regional Devolution and Social Policy* (Macmillan)
Crozier, Michel *The Stalled Society* (Viking)
Curwen, P. J. *Inflation* (Macmillan)
Dierkes, Meinolf & Bauer, Raymond (editors) *Corporate Social Accounting* (Praeger)
Djilas, Milovan *The New Class* (Thames & Hudson)
Drucker, Peter *The Age of Discontinuity* (Heinemann)
Fanon, Frantz *The Naked of the Earth* (Penguin)
Friedman, Milton *Capitalism and Freedom* (University of Chicago)
Galbraith, J. K. *The New Industrial State* (Hamish Hamilton), *Economics and the Public Purpose* (Penguin)
Gans, Herbert J. *People and Plans* (Penguin)
Goldsmith, Edward (editor) *Can Britain Survive?* (Sphere Books)
Hicks, John *The Crisis in Keynesian Economics* (Blackwell)
Hirsch, Fred *Social Limits to Growth* (Routledge & Kegan Paul)
Illich, Ivan *Deschooling Society* (Penguin)
Jencks, Christopher *Inequality* (Penguin)
Jenkins, David *Job Power* (Heinemann)
Jones, Aubrey *The New Inflation* (Penguin)
Kahn, Herman & Wiener, Anthony J. *The Year 2000* (Macmillan)
Kempner, Thomas, MacMillan, Keith & Hawkins, Kevin H. *Business & Society* (Allen Lane)
Keynes, J. M. *The General Theory of Employment, Interest and Money* (Macmillan)
Lekachman, Robert *The Age of Keynes* (Penguin)
Means, Gardiner C. et al. *The Roots of Inflation* (Wilton House)

BIBLIOGRAPHY

Mishan, E. J. *The Costs of Economic Growth* (Staples)

Myrdal, Gunnar *The Challenge of World Poverty* (Allen Lane)

Ortega y Gasset, José *The Revolt of the Masses* (Mentor)

Rawls, John *A Theory of Justice* (Oxford University)

Rees-Mogg, William *The Reigning Error* (Hamish Hamilton)

Robinson, Joan *Economic Philosophy* (Penguin)

Rome, Club of *The Limits to Growth* (Earth Island)

Rostow, W. W. *The Stages of Economic Growth* (Cambridge University)

Rueff, Jacques *Balance of Payments* (Macmillan)

Schumacher, E. F. *Small Is Beautiful* (Blond & Briggs)

Servan-Schreiber, J. J. *The American Challenge* (Penguin)

Shanks, Michael *The Stagnant Society* (Penguin), *The Innovators* (Penguin), *The Quest for Growth* (Macmillan)

Shonfield, Andrew *Modern Capitalism* (R.I.I.A./Oxford), *Europe: Journey to an Unknown Destination* (Penguin)

Stephenson, Hugh *The Coming Clash* (Weidenfeld & Nicolson)

Stewart, Michael *Keynes and After* (Penguin)

Titmuss, Richard M. *Income Distribution and Social Change* (Allen & Unwin), *Social Policy* (Allen & Unwin)

Toffler, Alvin *Future Shock* (Pan)

Vickers, Geoffrey *Value Systems and Social Process* (Penguin), *Freedom in a Rocking Boat* (Penguin)

Ward, Barbara and Dubos, René *Only One Earth* (Penguin)

Index